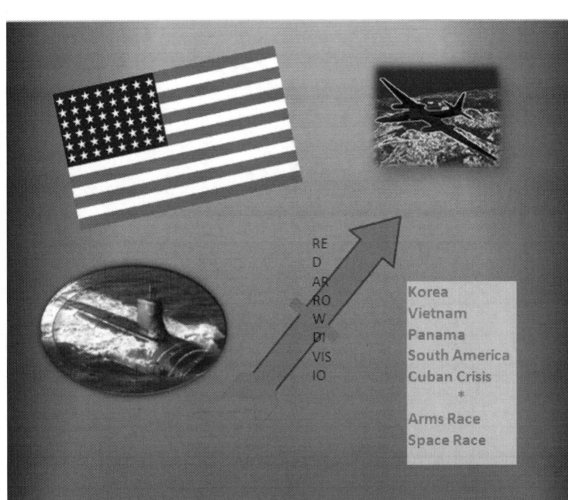

RE
D
AR
RO
W
DI
VIS
IO

Korea
Vietnam
Panama
South America
Cuban Crisis
*
Arms Race
Space Race

COUNTERFEIT PEACE
THE COLD WAR

THE WISCONSIN CONNECTION - BOOK TWO

THE VETERANS OF BEAVER DAM, WISCONSIN USE THEIR ACTUAL STORIES TO TELL OF EVENTS DURING THIS TIME PERIOD IN OUR HISTORY. BULLETPROOF READING AND STRANGER THAN FICTION THEIR WORDS WILL RESONATE WITH AND CHALLENGE THE READER. THIS BOOK IS NOT FOR THE FAINT OF HEART AS YOU ARE DRAWN INTO THE MINDSET OF THESE AMERICAN WARRIORS.

COMPILED AND WRITTEN BY: BOB FRANKENSTEIN

THE WISCONSIN CONNECTION (BOOK ONE)
RENDEZVOUS WITH HISTORY

INTERNET KEY WORDS
WW II—POWs—MIAs—Hitler—Nazi—Allies—Beaver Dam—Wisconsin

THE WISCONSIN CONNECTION (BOOK TWO)
Counterfeit Peace
The Cold War

KEY WORDS

Korea—Vietnam—Cold War—Cuban Crisis—Beaver Dam—

Wisconsin—Veterans—Berlin Wall—Iron Curtain

Remember the past or you will repeat it ...

Order this book online at www.trafford.com
or email orders@trafford.com

Most Trafford titles are also available at major online book retailers.

Printed in the United States of America.

ISBN: 978-1-4269-9715-0 (sc)
ISBN: 978-1-4269-9716-7 (e)

Library of Congress Control Number: 2011917954

Trafford rev. 10/24/2011

 www.trafford.com

North America & international
toll-free: 1 888 232 4444 (USA & Canada)
phone: 250 383 6864 ✦ fax: 812 355 4082

OUR COMMUNITY GOES TO WAR

Our struggle for freedom

Bob Frankenstein

WRITTEN AND ADAPTED FROM ACTUAL STORIES OF LOCAL VETERANS
BY BOB FRANKENSTEIN

COVERS THE COLD WAR (COUNTERFEIT PEACE) PERIOD
FEBRUARY 1945 TO AUGUST 1991

ACKNOWLEDGEMENTS

The author acknowledges with full humility and gratefully thanks this community of extraordinary people who were willing to share their historic stories and tears experienced during a very dangerous span of time called the "Cold War" or as some call it a period of a Counterfeit Peace.

For ten years this writer interviewed veterans asking them to share their emotions, their pictures, and their fears, which they did with a mixture of pride and sometimes a sense of shame. This book is created from their words and thoughts.

Some internet research was done to verify their stories and to obtain the public domain military pictures used to enhance their stories. Many pictures were actually their own pictures as they lived their part in history. If pictures or words slipped through that are used by others we veterans thank them for their use.

Beaver Dam, Wisconsin newspapers were researched to make this book as accurate as possible.

Dodge County Historical Society was also researched and will act as the final home for these individual pieces of military history as collected by the author.

This book would not have been possible without the encouragement and help of others in this community.

Heart-felt thanks to John Rabata for proof-reading this book and a very special thanks to my wife, Lorraine, for her patience.

DEDICATED TO THE GIs WHO NEVER RETURNED HOME

Many veterans gave their life so this author could write this book in a free country. Thousands of soldiers are considered still on active duty in prison camps, missing in action, or serving in limbo until they can be found and brought home.

This book and the stories inside are written by real veterans wishing to honor all veterans who gave so much during this period of counterfeit peace. Without their sacrifice, patience, determination, and loyalty we could easily be a colony of a communist nation.

INTRODUCTION

World War Two forced Communist countries and Democratic countries to work and fight together against their common foes, Nazi Germany, Fascist Italy, and Imperialist Japan. It was a matter of survival! However, we must first remember that the Soviet Union was at first an ally of Nazi Germany happily dividing up Poland as spoils of war. When Hitler's Germany betrayed and invaded the Soviet Union; the Soviet Union then switched sides thus forming an uneasy alliance with the Allies. This would play out in several ways, the greatest of which was the lack of trust, resulting paranoia, disputes on conducting the war, secret agreements, and lack of respect for partner country leaders. There was always an under-current with each of these uneasy politically opposed allies seeking an advantage over each other during and after the war. In other words the communist and democratic sides did not trust each other and sought a strategic advantage over each other.

*Adding to this intrigue, was the fact that political factions in the colonies of these warring nations demanded independence as a reward for helping win the war. Thus Formosa, (Taiwan) India, Korea, French Indo-China (Vietnam) (Palestine/Israel), Egypt, other colonies in Africa, South American countries and many other oil and mineral rich regions would be pawns to be haggled over after the war. Even critical areas like the Panama Canal Zone sought to be independent. If and when they won their independence would they be Communist or Democratic country friendly? So began a **Counterfeit Peace** the West calls the "Cold War" period in which newly formed floundering governments of these new independent states were violated by civil war and political upheaval much of which was staged by outside influence seeking a communist or democratic alliance.*

Several countries such as Germany, Poland, Korea, Vietnam, were partitioned or collectively controlled by the WW II winners leaving a festering open wound. As a consequence after WW II there would be several civil wars not so secretly supported by an aggressive Communist nation and a defensive Democratic nation. This would also be a struggle between two cautious superpowers not daring to directly challenge each other but using surrogates to harass each other. These breakouts of warfare were renamed a "Police Action" or "A Conflict" because an all-out war did not dare be declared as each side had the power to destroy the world. This time of counterfeit peace was used to acquire influence and control while democratic police actions were used to limit communist aggression and influence. These efforts were fought by; undermining governments, instigating revolt, fermenting civil war, and funding favorable elections. Friendly governments were cultivated by both sides to provide oil and critical minerals. Eventually this rivalry would even spread into a high tech race to control and gain superiority over all strategic of areas of the world; sky, land, oceans, and outer space. The communist countries focused on offensive war ability and a worldwide struggle to control minds while the democratic West focused on limiting the spread of influence and aggression of communist countries around the world.

Cold War insanity started in Yalta February, 1945 with a conference to set-up a working structure to manage the WW II losers even before the war ended.

The countries controlled by the French, British, and United States would prosper causing a mass exodus or brain drain from the communist world. The Eastern block of countries, including East Germany, would be eventually effectively cut off from the rest of the world and would fester under the Soviet Union wishing to prevent this ongoing exodus. North Korea would suffer the same fate under their communist leaders.

It was part of this façade or counterfeit peace that a small town community struggles with in Wisconsin. Beaver Dam, like every other small town would send its sons and daughters but would wage war in denial mode. Beaver Dam people were tired of war and weary of giving up the good things in life to the war effort in a faraway country. This is their story as told by the people who lived it.

It is time for you to slip quietly inside the minds of ordinary people of the small community of Beaver Dam, Wisconsin who are coping with a counterfeit peace, fighting wars undeclared, with goals undetermined, grievances unclear, issues unresolved, with the gory details neatly hidden safely underground in cemeteries. Join me as we walk in the shoes of heroes of this little community.

Korea

June 25, 1950, the Democratic People's Republic Of Korea (DPROK) (North Korea) (NK) opened fire on (the naive military forces of Republic Of Korea) (ROK) (South Korea) positions south of the 38th Parallel, the dividing line between the Soviet Union and Chinese supported communist government of North Korea and the United States supported democratic government of South Korea. This bombardment was followed with tank supported assaults across the 38th Parallel by North Korean infantry. North Korea had prepared well for war while South Korea did not. It was the beginning of months of open bloody combat, a tumultuous truce on July 27, 1953, then more localized bloodshed making Korea an official combat zone until January 1955. Finally more counterfeit peace!

First there must be US military and United Nations buildup and support system for these front line troops.

JOHN RABATA OF Beaver Dam was 17 years 3 months old when he enlisted in the U.S. Air Force on June 6th, 1949. His three year hitch would be extended by order of President Truman to an indefinite time period when the Korean Police Action or Korean Conflict broke out. He was assigned to the 3309th Research and Development Squadron (later renamed; The Human Resources Center) at Lackland Air Force Base, San Antonio, Texas. Selection for this elite organization required scores on the Stanine Tests which exceeded the 95 percentile.

Projects undertaken by this unit necessitated close cooperation between the military and the civilian psychologists who directed them. Duties also included (TDYs) temporary duty assignments to various pilot training bases in the southwest to administer psychomotor tests to ascertain the skills (or lack thereof) of cadets and officers aspiring to become pilots. In plain language they were to help evaluate the ability, mindset, and motor skill levels of military pilot candidates and to classify them as suitable or unsuitable for flight training.

John had many good experiences while in the service and feels it helped him prepare for life. He went on to college under the G. I. Bill leading to his life's work as an educator in Beaver Dam.

ISABELLE "IZZY" RICHARDSON lived on Long Island, NY during WW II, before eventually moving to Beaver Dam. While she was still in eighth grade she volunteered as a plane spotter from the roof of the local courthouse. When she saw a plane she would compare it to a picture system of known enemy and friendly planes and if she found a problem she had to report it to Civil Defense Authorities. It was her job to identify all planes entering the area.

At one time, she was also at Purdue University modeling the new (WAF) Woman's Air Force dress "blues" in a recruiting drive for the service. She thought the new ones looked "snappy". A "beautiful" hat topped it off. The WAF's early first uniforms had been men's army kakis.

1950, Izzy took aptitude tests and enlisted in the Air Force. She took more tests at Lackland Air Force Base to see what she qualified for. After basic, Izzy went to "Supply Technician School" at Lowery Field in Denver, Colo. It was here she had her picture taken with Bob Hope while he was at the base entertaining troops.

While she was training there, they had a funny thing happen. A man had been sent away on temporary duty and when he came back several months later he returned to his room in the barracks. It was late at night so he had no way of knowing it, but while he was gone the barracks was changed from a man's to a woman's barracks. He flew out of the building with well-aimed missiles pursuing him down the stairs and out the door. He was rescued by the MPs.

After her training, she was sent to Chanute, Ill., where she worked in a squadron supply room, and issued uniforms, etc. for a while. Izzy then transferred to a military plane parts supply room and issued repair parts, posted parts needed, did "hustling", ran errands, and much more.

During the Korean War, Izzy was stationed at Lackland Air Force Base. Many thousands of men were drafted, but the base only had quarters for only a portion of them so shelters had to be built under emergency conditions. Mothers vehemently complained because their drafted sons had to sleep on the ground. Located nearby was Kelly Field where the WAFs lived.

Izzy liked to visit the wounded in the hospital where the guys liked the attention helping them get though the day.

The hospital was so short of nurses that she was able to be transferred to the hospital. Normally the military will not approve transfers after you have been trained, but they really needed nurses.

She received on the job training as a Nurse's Aid and had to give penicillin shots, etc. One time Izzy had to deliver a baby in the emergency room all done without previous experience. She loved hospital work and took great pride in being a member of the service. She states: "Kids were inducted into the service, but confident men and women came out!"

December 5th, 1950, Beaver Dam newspaper front page! On the home front a high speed troop train carrying military troops and Christmas trees hit and destroyed a car with 4 local children and an adult driver in nearby South Beaver Dam. The driver (father of two of the children) lost control on an ice patch causing them to slide at an angle in front of the train. The high speed train cut off ¾ of their car leaving the drivers ¼ section intact. The four children were killed but the driver did not get a scratch. The incident was witnessed by **a** WW II veteran **Frank Engebretson** who was driving his car just behind the victims' car. He was deeply sickened by what he had seen.

Cora Manthe turned 21 years old during the Korean War era and was looking for adventure and a job after graduating from the University of Iowa. She took part in a three month summer tour of Europe with the National Student Association and upon returning received an invitation (with fourteen other girls) from Capital Airlines to apply for stewardess positions in Washington D. C. While waiting the results of her futile interview she started working for Hecht Department Store in Washington D. C.

As luck would have it, she heard about a government agency seeking college grads. She was soon hired by the Department of Defense, Armed Forces Security Agency Section, and sent to school for nine months after they did an extensive background check on her. She eventually would receive a "top secret clearance" and became a Research Analyst for several years. Her immediate supervisor was a Lt. Commander in the Navy. During her interview with this author she emphasized she could not talk about the work she did during this time.

She married a former Navy man and employment manager of Hecht Department Store after which they eventually moved to the Beaver Dam, Wisconsin area where he worked for the Wisconsin Department of Corrections and she owned an investment company.

Jan. 1951, **Bob's Schoenwetter** of Beaver Dam left for service from the armory in Beaver Dam traveling to Milwaukee with several friends who had enlisted with him. They wanted to have a chance to choose their service branch and to serve together.

They stayed at the Antlers Hotel while they processed after which they were sent by train to Lackland Air Force Base in Texas for basic training. In spite of a promise they would get to serve together Bob was separated from his friends and would take basic training with strangers. There was a huge draft call-up and influx of trainees for the Korean War so barrack housing for the trainees was at capacity hence they had to sleep on canvass cots in tents. They were issued two blankets but no mattress, so Bob bought local newspapers for insulation to keep warm. He was eventually transferred to Sewart Air Force Base in Tennessee to complete basic after which he was assigned to the 314th Supply Squadron. They maintained C-119 planes (Flying Boxcars) which were used to train paratroopers for airborne duty at nearby Fort Campbell.

While stationed there; Bob had the honor to be Honor Guard for President Truman when he dedicated the Atomic Energy Commission. They waited 3 hours on a hot day for the president to arrive and snapped to attention just as he stepped out of the plane. The President stopped to talk with Bob's buddy to his left asking him how he liked the service. Bob's buddy said, "Fine, but the food could be better". President Truman admonished him saying "He was lucky to have a bunk to sleep on". Bob said he will never forget this!

Eventually he was sent to Camp Stoneman, California for overseas assignment. He would be part of the vast support system needed to carry on the Korean War and believes he was singled out to go because the other man with an identical classification was married. While waiting for his ship to sail they were put on work details. One such detail was to unload 5 semi-loads of heavy quartered beef for the commissary. This assignment didn't last long because the sergeant forgot to take their dog tags . . . meaning he did not know who they were, so the first chance they got, they all slipped away while the sergeant was in the cooler. It was one furious sergeant who returned to their barracks and kidnapped more reluctant replacements. Bob said they got a lot of guff for bugging out, but now he was wiser and never hung around the barracks again.

They left Camp Stoneman by ship moving up to San Francisco for overseas shipment. They were leaving just as a ship load of Korean War returnees arrived. What an experience! The returnees were euphoric with joy, delighted to be coming home

LEAVING THE STATES—ALCATRAZ PRISON IN BACKGROUND

and the guys on Bob's ship glum and somber, so much so you could have heard a pin drop. Bob locked his misty eyes on Alcatraz until the island was lost from sight not wanting to think about leaving the states.

His uncle had suggested he find a bunk away from the ship's head (toilet) and that he take a supply of crackers in case of seasickness so he had a box of crackers stashed in his duffle bag. His mother had admonished him not to drink or smoke or he would do it when he returned home, so Bob chose not smoke giving away his free military cigarettes while in service. He learned to take care of himself and to take responsibility.

Bob was assigned to the 546th Ammo Supply Depot on Okinawa. The Air Force had three huge ammo dumps there and the Army had one. The men mused that if communist agents ever successfully detonated these massive monition dumps the island would simply disappear. Much of this ammo was destined for use in Korea.

When it came time for him to return to the States; he was one happy sergeant because sergeants don't pull (KP) kitchen duty on ship or so he thought. Surprise! Combat veterans returning from Korea had rank and respect so he had to wash pots and pans. His hands soon were cracking from the GI soap so a friendly medic in sick bay relocated him to making coffee the rest of the cruise.

Bob states; "Four years is a long time to be facing the unknown but as Bob Hope said "thanks for the memories."

Bob had a fear of flying so instead he came home on the train from San Francisco, California to South Beaver Dam, Wisconsin.

Gordon Laue of Beaver Dam said his tour of duty in Korea lasted eighteen months. He was stationed there from August 1950 until January 1951. He arrived in Korea after weeks in Japan waiting to be assigned. About this time the North Korean army had pushed the American and South Korean forces back into the "Pusan Perimeter".

He was assigned to the 6002 Maintenance Squadron, which was attached to the Eighteenth Fighter Bomber Wing. Their base was near Pusan and was called the military designation "K-9". It later became known as Dog Patch, Korea after the cartoon characters Lil Abner and Daisy Mae.

Their mission was to repair and maintain F-51 mustangs. The F-51 was a propeller driven plane which carried rockets and napalm. It was also armed with a fifty caliber machine gun.

One of the rituals performed at K-9 was the "Victory Roll". Whenever a pilot shot down an enemy plane he would do a victory roll upon his return. He would fly about fifty feet above the runway and do a complete roll-over of his plane.

When the fighting surged northward the 18th Wing was moved to K-10 near

F51 MUSTANG

Chinhae, where he was assigned as a crew chief for a F-51. Also, about this time there was a need for an advanced repair crew for which he volunteered. It consisted of 10 men and an officer, mostly specialists on F-51s. This team was to perform temporary repairs on disabled planes for a one time flight back to the main repair depot.

It was in November 1950, that they were sent to Pyongyang, North Korea. They were there about two weeks when the Chinese entered the war and they were forced to evacuate.

They retreated south to Suwon, (K-13) where they were introduced to "Bed Check Charlie". Every night about midnight he would fly low over the area in an obsolete bi-plane. Sometimes he would drop some bombs believed to be mortar rounds while the observer in the rear cockpit would strafe them with a burp gun. They were more or less nuisance raids to get them up and to keep them awake.

From Suwon, they went to K-16 near Yong Dung Po. It was there that he finished his tour of duty before coming back to the States. He arrived in San Francisco on Valentine Day, February 14, 1952.

Bob Jeske hadn't always lived in Beaver Dam. As a matter of fact, he had traveled throughout the world. After growing up on the North-side of Milwaukee, Bob had joined the Air Force serving for 20 years, 25 days. He had been stationed in various places around the world, including both the Pacific side and Germany during WWII. Later he moved to Beaver Dam, where he met June, his wife.

Bob Jeske was an Air Force field cook for eleven months while in Korea and provided chow to keep pilots and air crews well fed. The cooks lived in a quonset type hut and each worked their turn. Time off could be spent sleeping, playing cards, or mingling with the air crews. The following is taken from military unit records.

In September 1950, the 51st (FIG) Fighter Interceptor Group and its 16th and 25th Squadrons moved to Japan under operational control of the 8th Fighter Bomb Wing (FBW). Within hours of arrival, group pilots began flying F-80s on combat air patrol,

armed reconnaissance, and close air support missions over Korea. The 51st moved up to Kimpo Air Base, located just south of Seoul in October. In December it flew 763 sorties, including close air support for the 2nd Infantry Division cut off by the enemy in the vicinity of Kunu-ri. The 51st helped protect the division's flanks and destroyed enemy roadblocks halting southward movement. In early January 1951, to avoid being overrun by North Korean and

SUPPORT MISSIONS

Chinese forces it rejoined its parent wing in Japan, but continued to fly missions over Korea, staging first through Taegu and then through Suwon Air Base. Returning to Korea after the push back of North Korean and Chinese forces in late July, the 51st supported ground forces and its pilots flew patrol, escort, interdiction, and armed reconnaissance missions. In September and October, the group devoted its major combat effort against railroads and other main supply routes in North Korea. After the 51st transitioned to F-86 sabre jets in November-December, its primary mission became air superiority.

Unit role in Korean War from military records;

- *Moved from Naha to Itazuke Air Base, Japan in Sept. 1950 for operations over Korea.*
- *Relocated to Kimpo in early Oct. 1950 as North Korea Army retreated.*
- *Pilots engaged in first all jet air-to-air combat on 8 Nov. 1950.*
- *Chinese intervention forced the wing to retreat to Japan in Dec 1950.*
- *Using F-80s for ground attack missions destroyed over 7,000 buildings, 70 bridges, 500 railroad cars and 170 supply dumps.*
- *Switched to F-86 Sabre in late 1950 taking on air superiority mission.*
- *Relocated to Suwon air base in mid—1951 as North Koreans and Chinese pull back.*
- *Fourteen wing pilots became ACES with one becoming the leader in the war with 16 shoot-downs or kills.*
- *Wing fliers destroyed 307 MIGs and damaged 285 in aerial combat during the war. (14 enemy MIGs for every wing F-86 lost)*
- *Wing provided air defense after the cease-fire remaining in Korea until 1954 when it moved back to Naha AB, Japan.*

Junior Immerfall of Beaver Dam was drafted the latter part of WW II and was sent to Germany in 1946 where he served as a guard at a German prison of war camp for a year. When his tour of duty was over he reenlisted and when war broke out in Korea in 1950, he was shipped to Korea arriving in Pusan where he merged with the 7th Cavalry.

HOUSE TO HOUSE FIGHTING

About to be pushed into the sea, they formed the Pusan perimeter. After some desperate times pressure on them was relieved by the United Nations successful

THE IRON WARRIOR CALLED THE TANK

invasion of Inchon. The North Korean Army now cut-off from supplies and trapped between Pusan and Inchon fled north-east. United Nation troops pursued them up past Seoul and along the 38th Parallel clear up to the Chin Chin Reservoir in North Korea. Tanks would support them during the day, but had to with-draw each night to avoid being destroyed by infiltrators.

On Oct. 14th Chinese Communist Forces quietly crossed the Yalu River Border with China into North Korea to support the North Korean People's Army. By November four huge Chinese Communist armies were pounding United Nation troops during which fighting was so intense that ten Chinese Communist Divisions were so devastated they could never see action again in the war.

COVERING THE BACKS OF
RETREATING TROOPS

Note! Our air force flew into North Korea and over China in spite of public announcements limiting the war to Korea. Enemy planes taking off even a few feet above the ground or in the sky near or just over the border were considered fair game.

In turn the enemy would claim all planes were flown by North Korean pilots in spite of visual claims by our pilots that Soviet or Chinese pilots were flying some fighter planes. Chinese or the Soviet Union soil was never formally violated because no boots were ever set on their homeland soil proper nor were any military targets hit. In turn our military supply and support bases located in Japan were never attacked thus limiting the conflict only to Korea. These technicalities made it possible to politically limit expanding the war into a possible new world war.

By November 30th, 1950, the 1st Marine and 7th Infantry were trapped, encircled, and cut-off in the Chosin Reservoir area of North Korea by the huge Chinese Army. Things became so desperate that President Truman even considered the use of the atomic bomb against the Chinese army.

Lawrence Soldner of Beaver Dam was a part of this push into North Korea and the disastrous retreat. He would have his lungs severely damaged during this catastrophic event. Hundreds of soldiers would freeze to death on both sides. Thousands of men would also disappear and be labeled (MIAs) missing in action during the UN collapse on the west side of Korea and the fighting retreat of UN soldiers on the east side in their drive to the North Korean Port Hungnam and eventual evacuation.

BRINGING HOME THE DEAD AND WOUNDED

December 11-December 24. The evacuation of Hungnam involved withdrawal of most UN forces on the eastern side of North Korea. In a little over two weeks, about

THE SAD PLIGHT OF REFUGEES

a hundred-thousand military personnel, 17,500 vehicles and 350,000 tons of cargo were pulled out. In comparison with the undisciplined rout in central and western Korea little was left behind. Some 91,000 refugees also fled North Korea through the Hungnam sea-lift.

January 3, 1951, Now it was the Chinese and North Korean forces who would push and capture their way deep into the South. They were out for revenge and massacred anyone they thought helped or sympathized with the South.

Alvin Steffen of Beaver Dam started his military career serving in Italy in WW II. Years later he would

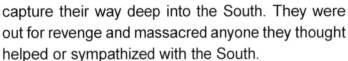

DELAY ACTION—BOMBED BRIDGE AND MACHINE GUNNERS SLOW THE ENEMY PROTECTING RETREATING UN TROOPS

SETTING EXPLOSIVES UNDER THE BRIDGES...
SOON TO BE DESTROYED TO PREVENT ENEMY CROSSINGS AFTER UN TROOPS HAD CROSSED

be serving actively in the Korean War. When Seoul was again to be overrun and abandoned he was an (MP) Military Policemen risking his own life to evacuate vehicles and men out of Seoul and is credited as being last man out of Seoul before it was overrun.

Retreating United Nation forces were told to use every means possible to avoid capture by the

North Korean and Chinese forces. They rode tanks, guns, vehicles of any description, anything headed south, to get out of there.

The United Nations were frantically rebuilding, retraining, and resupplying the men who had returned from central and western North Korea. They had abandoned much their equipment to the enemy as they retreated from overwhelming numbers of Chinese supporting North Korean forces.

February 14th, 1951, United Nation forces changed battlefield technics. Intelligence concerning location, numbers, and equipment had been somewhat lax because several field commanders looked down on their counterparts considering them to be

CLEARING MINES

only second class leaders. Cocky commanders in the field traveled openly on mountainous roads going blindly into traps set by communist forces. Wily enemy forces in turn traveled at night staying off the roads and dug in hiding during the day relying on arms and armor that could be carried by their own men or captured from retreating United Nation forces.

Up until now United Nation forces had tied themselves to roads in this country of mountains relying on tanks, heavy trucks, and artillery to carry on the war. The enemy who appeared out of nowhere merely blew up bridges, or front and rear vehicles of a column thus blocking the road and escape. Trapped United Nation soldiers forces were slaughtered like sitting ducks with heavy fire from the hills around them.

FREEZING...DOG-TIRED SOLDIERS

Now . . . military intelligence specialists studied the opposing commanders and troops seeking their weaknesses and soon discovered that the enemy usually carried supplies for about a three day battle and then had to resupply, withdraw, or die. They also did not adapt well to changing field conditions because

MOVING FORWARD

WAR DESTRUCTION

they were required to follow orders from remote commanders in North Korea or China. From that point on United Nation troops were determined to hold their ground knowing they could outlast an enemy offensive. They also realized that if United Nation combat

HAMMERING THE ENEMY

outposts were set on high ground and set 500 to 2500 yards in front of the United Nation main line of resistance that the enemy was forced to hit and knock out these outposts first (in order to protect their backside) when trying get at United Nation positions. These small but very effective combat outposts were used to suck in enormous concentrated human wave formations of the enemy, setting them up for attack by artillery, tanks, air power, and massive ship guns thus they could annihilate a much larger enemy force by using good communication with air and artillery support forces. This bait and annihilate method was the turning point used to walk the United Nation forces back north over a carpet of dead or captured masses of North Korean Peoples' Army and Chinese Communists Forces.

March 18, 1951, United Nation Forces moved to retake Seoul. **Lester Giese** of Beaver Dam was a part of the struggle to retake, and keep Seoul. Lester describes it this way. "There were so many bodies strewn in the streets that we were forced to throw them into the river. The river turned blood red and contained so many piled up floating bodies we had to use long poles to push them down and under the bridges so they could float out to sea".

The weather was always a major part of each battle. Springtime brought monsoons that washed out the roads, soaked them to the skin, and ruined food rations. Wintertime brought snow, bone chilling cold, and freezing hands and feet. During the conflict,

RETAKING GROUND MEANT MORE PRISONERS
(POWS)

clothes and supplies were many times unavailable so they had to make do. **Junior Immerfall**, a rifle squad leader from Beaver Dam, told his 14 people to put their socks inside around their belly to warm and dry them. They struggled together to keep warm, dry, and alive. "We had to help each other to stay alive," he said. He was wounded April 28th, 1951, in Seoul, Korea. After recovery, he returned to the United States and became a guard at Fort Leavenworth. He was discharged in 1952 after serving 5½ years. He received six battle stars and a Purple Heart.

June 13, 1951, United Nations troops reach and stabilize a Main Line of Resistance roughly along the 38th parallel. Thousands of additional United Nation troops would be killed or injured during this time of stalemate. There were many combat outposts set on various hills and mountain tops just ahead of the Main Line of Resistance again used to entice and then annihilate human wave charges by overwhelming communist forces.

July 10th, 1951 truce talks begin! When there was an impasse or the enemy side did not get what something they wanted, there would be a brutal attack or artillery barrage by enemy forces. The United Nations stood firm with no further escalation on their part, but chose to hold the line at all costs.

Life on the Main line of Resistance or in plain talk the "front line" was very difficult. It could include long hours of waiting and boredom or you might be struggling to construct a shooting or defensive position in tree roots, mud, solid rock or frozen ground. All positions had to include a heavy dirt or sand bag roof section if possible to protect inhabitants from hand or rifle grenades and incoming mortar rounds or deadly artillery shells with proximity fuses on them. These fuses had

MORTAR FIREBASE

settings on them so they could be set to explode the shell at different heights above the ground thus the shell shrapnel would effectively blast down into trenches and scatter injury or death over a larger area. Note! Mortar rounds are lopped in or out using a high arc and can be fired from a trench or vehicle. This high arc enables it to drop almost straight down into trenches, foxholes, or behind walls as compared to artillery which has a much flatter

trajectory fired from many miles away. A portable firing tube with a closed bottom is used to fire mortars rounds of several types, the round is dropped down the tube, hits a firing device at the bottom, and is propelled in a short high arc into the enemy positions.

TYPICAL MORTAR FIRING TUBE

Artillery barrages far exceeded anything ever seen in WW II. It was not unusual for shelling to be so intense that a thousand rounds or more would

JUNE 18, 1953 OUTPOST HARRY
FOUR DAYS OF FIGHTING - BRASS
SHELLS COLLECTED FOR THE
ORDINANCE DEPOT TO REUSE AGAIN

hammer small U.N. positions in ten or fifteen minutes followed with an enemy assault of hundreds and hundreds of men. These massive enemy formations terrorized the smaller United Nations or Republic of Korea outposts or positions. However, U.N. ships and artillery in turn would pour in heavy return fire taking advantage of these dense human waves of enemy men . . . annihilating them. The U.N. now owned the sky over Korea thus enabling fire and munitions from the sky to decimate them even more.

You must also endure very hot or freezing weather mixed with mud, rain, or snow. The terror of incoming shells, annoying enemy propaganda, total lack of privacy, and sporadic water, food and munitions supply will wear on you.

You live with the fear of close personal close combat, the fear of capture, the fear of dying, and the fear of being overrun and cut-off.

You also live with the sight and smell of the violent death of animals, children, women, and men. If a comrade is killed or wounded next to you in the trench, it might be possible to get them to the rear, but not so with those caught in no-man's land. (the area

BATTLESHIP USS WISCONSIN FIRING ON A TARGET IN KOREA

between the front-lines) Snipers were usually waiting to pick off would be rescuers or body recovery patrols.

Early morning brings flies and maggots while nights entice hungry animals. Soon after each battle it might be necessary to creep out into the open to roll these fermenting bodies down the hill or mountainside or remove them to be buried if possible. Snipers were usually waiting to take advantage of this.

If you were ordered to do a dreaded patrol, it meant crossing the booby-trapped and mined no-man's land between where you are dug-in and the enemy lines across the way. Your mission this night might cost you and your mates their lives if it not done efficiently, quietly, and very carefully to avoid discovery. A patrol encounter with the enemy must be dispatched with silently; using a knife, bayonet, or broken neck to prevent detection and alarm. Your mission might be to locate an enemy ammo dump, a certain gun emplacement, capture an enemy prisoner to interrogate, or remove mines for a push the next day. When your mission is complete you carefully make your way back toward home until you are challenged with the day's code sign. God help you if you don't return the correct counter sign for the day!

HOT TO GO

The author received this letter about **Eugene Wadleigh** of Beaver Dam who was in **Ed Paulsen's** squad while in Korea. The dog was called "Hot to Go". He was a Japanese Husky someone picked up while they were in Japan. He would become their mascot so they smuggled him to Korea where he served with them.

Gene and Ed shared a "home" at the front. It was nothing more than a ditch that had been widened and covered with steel fence posts and sand bags. A shelter half (half a tent) served as a door.

HOME SWEET HOME

In the background you can see that a mortar round had exploded nearby. Also note that all of the trees are blown away . . . . just sticks protruding. They also survived 20 below weather.

They couldn't stand up in their home and had to crawl in or out on hands and knees. Rats invaded their home while they were relaxing on their sleeping bags one day. A rat peeked into the door so Gene said, "Move your foot". Ed did and Gene shot the rat

OUR TROPHY "RAT"

with a .30 caliber bullet. They both posed with the rat. Ed included a picture of himself holding the rat.

Gene was not only one of his squad members, but Ed considered him as a friend. Ed knew that he could count on him. Ed states they had lots of idle time on their hands at the front, at times. They talked, and Gene told him that he had worked for the Jolly Green Giant cannery. Ed believes Gene said that he supervised women, and Gene told him that he enjoyed his work. Gene said that the women were good workers. **Ed Paulsen** (Squad Leader) (Minnesota)

Forrest "Bud" Snow of Beaver Dam enlisted in the Naval Reserves about 1948 in Chicago, Ill. while he was still in school. His unit was called to active duty in January

MILITARY TAXI & DELIVERY SERVICE

1951. He reported to Great Lakes Naval Station for boot training. Boot training completed, he was sent to Naval Air Station, Norfolk, Virginia in April 1951. He was assigned to Air Transport Squadron 22. While there, he was reassigned to Aviation Storekeepers School, Jacksonville, Florida. Upon completion, he returned to his old assignment in squadron 22 and remained there until his discharge in 1954.

With the onset of the Korean War and the need for increased Fleet logistic support, VR-22 became Fleet Tactical Support Squadron 22 in December 1950 and assumed a Carrier Onboard delivery mission. The squadron had been flying Sky-Trains and almost immediately received the first TBM-3R Avengers. (TBM Avengers made naval aviation history during World War II as a carrier—based torpedo bomber) (The TBM-3R had been modified to carry seven passengers and a ton of cargo) He occasionally made emergency military supply flights with critical components and parts to anywhere in the world.

Area soldiers killed or missing in action in Korea from Beaver Dam and Dodge County

Norbert J. Gorman KIA July 31st, 1950   **Ronald M. Zirbel** July 31st, 1950 (MIA)
Donald Albert August 30th 1951 (MIA)   **Kenneth Mellenthien** KIA Aug. 30, 1951
Jerrold Fronzowiak KIA October 9th, 1951   **Melvin L. Kuehl** KIA July 31, 1952.
Carl C. Slade KIA November 17, 1952   **Glenn E. Kohn** KIA July 24, 1953.

Arnold R. Wodill was drafted in 1952 and received basic training in the 3rd Armored Division at Fort Knox, Kentucky.

He shipped out to Korea after basic training and upon arrival he was assigned to the 25th Infantry Division, 14th Infantry Regiment, Company M.

Their orders were to perform a blocking action against the enemy. They were dug in about a mile in front of their field mess area so each night someone from each squad would to go back to the mess area for drinking water. Arnie felt he was over there to do his part so he volunteered to do this.

Life was very basic. Improvised outdoor toilets were part of life and electric power was a dream.

HEART BREAK RIDGE

When they received orders to move up to the frontline his squad leader was in need of an assistant for which he was chosen. An assistant gunner was also needed when they moved up and he was chosen for that, too. They remained on the front line until the truce was signed.

Eventually, he went to N.C.O. (non-commissioned officers) school and was promoted to sergeant when he graduated.

He took an extension in Korea and received another stripe. In all, he was there about 18 months. He came home as a sergeant first class and is proud of these promotions.

He stated, "I never got wounded and I didn't get any special medals except the combat infantry badge and various Korean and overseas service medals."

Upon returning to the states and home, he entered the Reserves. He was promoted to Master Sergeant while in the Reserves and holds permanent rank of E-7. He received his honorable discharge in 1964.

Note! (The following is from Division records] When truce negotiations began to fail, the 25th Division assumed the responsibility of guarding the approaches of Seoul on May 5, 1953. Twenty three days later, a heavy Chinese assault was hurled at them, but the Division held its ground and the assault was repulsed. The brunt of the attack was absorbed by the 14th Infantry while successfully defending Seoul from continued attack from May to July 1953.

Again negotiators labored toward an elusive truce.

The 14th Infantry Regiment was subjected to almost constant combat especially along the 38th Parallel defending places like "The Punchbowl" and "Pork Chop Hill".

Leon Neis of Beaver Dam went into the service Oct. 1952. He was inducted at Fort Sheridan and went to Fort Knox for basic training.

About April of 1953, he shipped out via Seattle, Washington, where he boarded the General C.C. Ballou headed for Korea. ("General" class troopships could carry up to 5600 troops, officers, nurses, and doctors plus crew.) About 23 days later, he arrived off the coast of Korea and landed at Inchon where he became a part of the 2nd Infantry Division, 23rd Regiment, Easy Company.

GENERAL C.C. BALLOU

One night the North Koreans made a push toward their main line of resistance (MLR). The brass (military officers) feared the enemy might break through their lines (his outfit had the privilege to be in reserve a few miles in the rear at the time) so they received orders to move up to the front as reinforcements to prevent a break-through. It rained continuously as they moved up in the dark. They stayed there for about 24 hours before returning about 1 AM the next night, muddy, wet, and cold. They were

DINNERTIME IN THE REAR

vainly trying to bunk down in a tent that held about 20 men but their feet were so swollen they could not remove their combat boots.

There was swearing coming from the front of the tent where an Indian Master Sergeant was looking for a man to volunteer for kitchen policing duty (KP) at 3 AM. The men just snarled at him as he worked his way back toward Leon asking each man as he walked by. When he asked Leon if he would be willing to do KP Leon answered in the affirmative and asked what time did he need to get up? He was told 3 AM or in about 2 hours. The grateful sergeant's problem was solved.

About a week later, the sergeant confided to Leon he had been instructed to find a rifleman who deserved to be in the 4th platoon and that is when he remembered the favor Leon did for him. He now was returning the favor by selecting Leon to be promoted to the 4th weapons platoon. Eventually Leo was even promoted to leader of the 4th platoon before he left Korea.

A friend of Leon remembers seeing a wounded soldier brought back to camp. Before the war the young man had hoped to be a professional skater, however with the mortar damage to his legs, it was evident he would never realize his dream.

Another friend and his buddy recall crossing a river in the dead of night to retrieve food rations for their company. One ended up helping the other who was desperately struggling to survive in the cold water.

Leon recalls the importance of prayer despite seeing war going on around him. The rosary he made by tying knots in a string was well worn from use.

"The bond between you and your buddies is close," Leon said "You put your life in their hands." This trust begins in basic training and continues until discharge. It extends through night watch duties while your buddies sleep, to sharing rest and recuperation leave in a foreign city.

MORTAR OUTPOST

Indeed, taking cover in the same foxhole, hearing the whistle of shells pass overhead, has a sobering effect on even the toughest man. It is scary! You don't know whether or when you're going to get hit. "We all got a good taste of being scared" Leon said. "At the same time, that fear heightened simple pleasures".

He and his friends gleefully remember moving back from the lines and retrieving a cold can of beer that they had tied down in a cool stream.

"Tents pitched on rocky ground, the sounds of war, and reading by candlelight provided an indescribable eeriness", Leon added. It's a feeling shared among soldiers willing to do their part. "We were there for a purpose," "We were there for freedom".

But with war came much uncertainty. "The worst part is the unknown" he said. "When you move up to prepare for a counter attack, you do not know the situation".

As the months passed, there was hope for peace.

His platoon was a heavy weapons platoon, consisting of mortars, Browning automatic rifles, heavy and light machineguns, bazookas, etc. Soldiers of this platoon do not go on patrol at night in enemy territory, one of the most fearsome of details you might have to do.

THE CHORWAN VALLEY

He spent much of his combat time positioned in the Chorwan Valley along the main line of resistance (MLR) with the enemy MLR was just across the way. It was this "no man's land" between which was pushed back and forth with each side seeking to gain an advantage before a ceasefire was signed. Night patrols harassed the enemy and shelling each other was a part of life. The enemy sought their weaknesses in turn. Searchlights and trip-wire flares illuminated a part of many nights to keep the each other at bay.

Their outposts Bubble, Tom, Dick, all nearby, and Poppa-san Hill held by the enemy, all looked down on the river and valley below.

Occasionally Korean folks ventured out to work the land or to scrounge for food. Koreans civilians were frequently used to dig and enlarge foxholes or to construct sandbag positions.

One of the ironies of this war was the lack of supplies. Many times the only way UN troops could get more ammo or shells was to turn in spent ones from previous engagements. That meant many soldiers and any civilians working with them were out looking for spent munitions to exchange for a new supply needed for the next battle. This work had great risk because of minefields and snipers hidden throughout the valley and on the roads. Thank God, the U.N. Air Force cut and hampered the enemy supply lines as well.

Tanks did not work well in rice paddies or on the sides of mountains so they were frequently dug in and used as artillery. Tanks, when used to push ahead, had to be pulled back behind the lines at night to prevent them being destroyed by the enemy.

Leon took one R & R (Rest & Recuperation) leave to Fukuoka, Japan. These trips were provided by the military to help combatants relax and to prevent battle fatigue.

Once a week Leon took the time to walk a mile or two back past the field chow line to attend church services rain or shine each Sunday. Church consisted of a white sheet on the hood of a jeep and a chaplain.

One day a young man from New York and from a different company, came up to him and stated he wanted to become a Christian and asked him if he would be his sponsor. Leon was pleased to do this for him and considered it an honor. The young man was baptized and soon had the needed papers signed, but now Leon was curious. He asked the young man how he had picked him, a total stranger, to be his sponsor? The young man didn't hesitate, "All I had to do was watch who went to church every Sunday". "That's how I knew who would be the right person to ask".

CHURCH SERVICE ON A JEEP

No one wants to be the last soldier injured or killed in a war! "God . . . when are they gonna sign that truce?" was beating in the mind of every GI in Korea. Oddly on the evening of the July 27th the enemy hit an ammunition dump.

The truce was signed and both MLRs fell back and formed the (DMZ) Demilitarized Zone on 27th July 1953. Finally, Leon's prayers were answered! When the truce was signed soldiers from both sides cautiously emerged from caves and shelters to wave at each other. He left Korea by way of Inchon about June of 1954 and returned home by way of San Francisco Oct. of 1954.

John Omen of Beaver Dam completed basic training at Fort Knox, Kentucky in 1952. He was sent to Seattle, Washington where he would board a ship for Korea. Twenty eight days later he arrived at Inchon, South Korea. His group would join up with the 7th Infantry Division. The

OLD BALDY

battles of; Old Baldy, Suicide Hill, Death Valley, and Westview Outpost would consume nine months of his life. Westview would be John's last battle before the cease fire. John speaks of the time when they were relaxing that a soldier nearby fell silent. When John turned to look he discovered the soldier had been shot in the head by a sniper unseen and unheard. Twenty minutes before 11 AM on July 27, 1953, a message was received by the Division and immediately relayed to all units that a truce had been signed and was to go into effect at ten o'clock that night. The men breathed a sigh of relief and each man prayed silently that his luck would hold out just another twelve hours.

On Outpost Westview, where a 1-1/2 hour battle had erupted the night before, anxious men now wondered if the enemy might decide to finish with a final barrage of fire. Who would be the last man to die? Minute by minute 12 hours of waiting slowly dragged by.

UN SEARCH LIGHT TRUCK

About 8:45 PM an order was passed from man to man: "No firing from now on unless they start it. It's up to them!" Around 9:00 PM the communists taunted their hopes when a huge searchlight began working the face of Old Baldy. Finally someone hopefully whispered to a buddy, "Look, they finally killed that damned searchlight." Another exultant soldier hopefully exclaimed, "We gonna make it!" Then they could hear joyous voices across the line and for the first time violence of war vanished. All went weirdly quiet! It was 10 PM and their inhumane life in Korea had just come to an end.

Euphoria spread throughout Korea and across the United Nation's world, but soon it would be tempered by continued North Korean and Chinese belligerence and betrayal.

John got a much needed R&R to Japan. Later, when he returned to the states he was sent to Fort Carson, Colorado where he was a mess sergeant until his discharge in 1953. He sent to Korea as a Pvt. and returned a Sgt.

Richard Neuman joined the Army in Aug. of 1953. When he left for camp he ended up at Fort Riley, Kansas. After a short stay there, he found himself at Fort Leonard Wood, Missouri for eight weeks of infantry training.

He then was put into the Army Corp of Engineers for 16 more weeks of training, which included different types of bridge building, mine laying and removal, setting and removing booby traps. During these months of training he had fired expert on the rifle ranges with the M-I, and the M-1 Carbine, and Machine Guns; 30 Caliber and 50 Caliber. He was then put on a machine gun squad, and they would then fire in competition with other units. Sometime during this time period he discovered that the average life of a machine gunner was counted in minutes during a battle so he somehow fired badly the next several times out, and was then removed from the team.

He sometimes was assigned to Prisoner Chaser Duty, which consisted of taking prisoners through training and many other duties.

During this time many of the guys returning from Korea were put in their company awaiting their discharge. Among these was a Sgt. Hoff who was a bulldozer operator. He got the okay to train Dick in bulldozer operation and soon Dick was assigned full time duty on the dozer.

Dick did a lot of road work, but still had to go through repeat training exercises. His biggest assignment was when he had to build an underwater bridge across a large deep river. It had to be built so it could not be spotted from the air. After a fly-over inspection and a General was driven over it, he was told he had passed with flying colors.

He then was made an instructor and spent much of his time training guys from other companies, National Guard, and Reserve trainees.

In the summer of 1954 they were sent to Fort McCoy to help train National Guard and Reserves trainees. One training incident stands out above the rest. About 20 of them were sent to help a Reserve unit build a bridge across a river. Upon arriving they found the bridge parts as well as about eight reserve officers. They built the bridge while the reservists sat in the shade and drank beer. The only time they were on the bridge was to take pictures of them being thrown into the water from the bridge. Several weeks later we received a copy of their home town newspaper showing their pictures on the front page, with the head line: Local Reserves Build Bridge at Fort McCoy. After a few more episodes similar to the one just mentioned they were sent back to Fort Leonard Wood.

A short time after their return he received his Corporal stripes which he felt he earned by trying to teach those Guards and Reserves how to operate a dozer. He continued training guys with operating a dozer until the time of his discharge which came 2 months early because the Army was downsizing now that the truce in Korea looked like it would hold together.

Overall he says, he had grown up, and learned an awful lot about things he never would have learned had he not gone in. After he was out for a time, he joined the National Guards for a year and got out with the rank of Sergeant.

WORK-HORSE OF THE MILITARY—D-9 BULLDOZER

In the summer of 1953, Donald Soldner of Beaver Dam was trained on heavy equipment at Fort Leonard Wood. He was then sent to Greenland where he would work until time for discharge. He was a seaport dock crane operator loading and unloading military ships.

This next story is a little longer and is used by the writer to create a bigger picture of service in a war zone during this counterfeit peace.

January 1954, Bob Frankenstein's father took him to catch the chartered military bus at the old Beaver Dam Armory. He was 17 years old and it was his draft date. When he said goodbye to his dad, his Dad had tears in his eyes. The bus took him to Milwaukee, where he had his medical and was "sworn in" and then on to Fort Leonard Wood for six months of serious training. He was very uneasy!

"Buck" Rahn of Beaver Dam also left for service on that day.

Bob was assigned to Charlie Company, 6th Armored Division. He went to bed at ten PM and got up three or four in the morning on many days. He had toothpaste to brush his teeth, shaving equipment, real cotton sheets, haircuts, underwear, nice uniform, and new friends. He was learning fast and was put on a drill team. He had never had it so good and even made Soldier of the Month! The Army made him a carpenter and explosives specialist in the combat engineers. Cadre (all Korean combat veterans) focused on close combat training, bayonet training, accurate shooting, and no non-sense battlefield training.

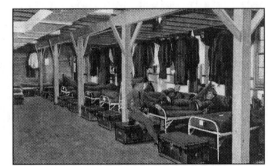
FORT LEONARD WOOD BARRACK LIFE

He also finished High School through the University of Wisconsin. His Mother and Dad had been ill for over a year forcing him to stay home from school and work the farm with his brothers and sisters. His mother died Sept. 1953. High final grades from the UW Wisconsin made him eligible for a diploma from Beaver Dam High School.

He tried to make it home about once a month on a weekend pass. One weekend he was hitchhiking home (About 550 miles each way) with a trucker who fell asleep. They went off the road, rolled end over end several times and careened sidewise to a stop. Bob was knocked unconscious and woke up on top of the trucker, but eventually made it home in time to stand up for his Dad's wedding!

During his advanced explosives training period, Bob occasionally was given a special armed detail. He was ordered to escort soldiers unfit for duty (criminals, thieves, murderers) around Fort Leonard Wood getting them dishonorable discharge papers and "Jody" suits. They were not allowed to dishonor the uniform and so were given these ugly Jody suits to wear to the post gate. Just outside the front gate of Fort Leonard Wood, Bob would officially release his prisoner and a civilian sheriff or police officer would immediately arrest the man.

Late July 1954, after basic and advanced training, most of his company and friends received (so-called) secret orders to Korea. His group was sent to the post dentists where fillings were done on even slightly stained teeth. Bob's teeth were in excellent condition but they filled seven or eight of them anyway. When he protested . . . they said, "You don't want a toothache in a combat zone".

Then they were flown to a base near Tacoma, Washington by chartered Ozark Airlines and after a couple of days, (departure a secret) he was shipped to Korea on the General Mitchell. It took nineteen days at sea to get to Japan by going over the top of the world by way of Alaska. They had about 4500 men, plus 300 nurses, and the crew of sailors on board ship. The ship could carry about 5600 troops. Their ship did submarine

GENERAL MITCHELL

PACKED LIKE SARDINES

BATTLE STATIONS DRILL

and air raid drills with targets and live ammo several times on the way over. They also made a stop at Yokohama, Japan where he spent August 19th, 1954 on shore leave. He made a phone call back home to his brother to wish him; "Happy Birthday", then back to sea for a few days.

They could smell land long before they could see it. Korea was a land of mountains, water buffalo, honey (human waste) wagons, and rice paddies. It was also totally decimated by war.

The days after leaving Japan and before they docked at Pusan, South Korea, they were given very short combat zone haircuts, training in case of capture by the enemy, Korean culture orientation, and issued field clothing and combat gear. Early morning as they left the ship; arms, ammo, rations, and canteen water were issued. They were also warned that if they lost their rifles (serial numbers were recorded) they would have to pay for them and that their canteen of water had to last them at least 18 hours. When they off-loaded they were hauled by "cattle truck" (open semi—truck) through Pusan to the railroad depot.

They were sent north by way of railroad to Yong Dung Po. The steam engine

TRAIN TO YONG DUNG PO

train stopped often on the way providing an opportunity for women and orphan children with missing limbs, eyes, and empty stomachs to beg or sell things at the open windows. War, shelling, land mines, and grenades had taken their toll! Late that night they moved from Yong Dung Po through Seoul traveling about two hours still further north by truck to an outpost over-looking a river crossed with newly built vehicle and railroad bridges with a nearby tiny village below them.

The next morning Company Officers ordered them not to ever salute them outdoors or where it might be seen. He became part of 2nd platoon of the 62nd Combat Engineer Battalion. Each platoon was assigned different duties such as; protect the bridges, guard the compound, build and repair roads, build military equipment shipping crates, rifle cases and wheel blocks, or construct quonsets for a mess-hall, orderly room, supply room, and motor repair shop before the coming winter

HIDDEN 62ND ENGINEER OUTPOST ON TOP OF HILL IN THE FAR BACK OF PICTURE

while acting as an outpost. Bob was assigned to construct shipping cases and railroad wheel blocks for units moving out working 12 hour shifts while one squad stood guard.

They were somewhere near the line created by the truce, but did not know exactly where they were. They just followed orders!

2ND PLATOON TENTS

September 4th, 1954,
within days after arriving in camp, a Navy P2V was shot down by MIGs putting their outpost on full alert! Welcome to Korea!

KEEPING SAFE

Snakes, combat rations, and very very dark nights became a part of his life. He was well, slept in a nine man tent and showered in a nearby sheltered gully about every ten days or so. Water was hauled in by a tank truck. The truck had several shower nozzles mounted on it charged with a pump for pressure, and a built in water heater. (it didn't work) They stood on wooden pallets while showering. There was no privacy and shower time was very short. Someone was always on guard while others showered. Soiled uniforms were sent down to the village for Momma-san to wash and iron by hand. An outhouse was located central point and was emptied once a week by escorted Korean civilians and hauled away using a water buffalo and honey wagon.

WASHING CLOTHES BY THE RIVER

Treated drinking water (trucked in from a water point) came from a canvas leister bag. Combat rations made during WW II could have been fresher and better tasting. Supplies and mail were brought once or twice a week.

He lived and slept with a rifle and felt important for the first time in his life. If he did well he was rewarded, if he did something reckless or foolish, he was firmly chewed out. He had to learn fast because Korea was very unforgiving.

There were a few men who would sneak down to the village looking for the companionship of a woman. One night two of these men fought over the attention of the same woman. They actually managed to slit each other's throat with one almost dying, the other seriously injured. After hospitalization, both were sent to the stockade for 3 months. When they returned, one had a fearsome looking five inch scar and the other a wide four inch long scar in the throat area.

KOREAN VILLAGE

He did like the Korean people. They lost everything in the war, but were courageous and worked hard. They struggled; rebuilding their homes of mud with rice straw roofs, planting rice to feed their starving people, gathering something to burn to heat their tiny homes, while franticly looking for lost children and family.

After the truce was signed; it was time for the pent up anger "to get even" and to "root out" North Korean sympathizers. (Not always pretty!) Body remains from the war were found in ditches while rebuilding roads, in collapsed buildings, in rice paddies, and most anything might be booby trapped with live military weapons from either side. Sadly children were curious players of these new toys.

Korea was now a war-torn wasteland that did not hesitate to bite the very young or naïve newcomer.

Bob was struck with the fact that the women hid their identity by wearing the same white loose clothes as the men until it dawned on him that they wanted to avoid being raped! However, women with war babies frequently carried and nursed their young openly while working in the rice paddies. It would be many months later however that these hesitant women started to wear pretty traditional dress.

Combat Kelly (a combat veteran) told them this story about a South Korean nurse who gave aid to the wounded on both sides. When the United Nations pushed the North Koreans and Chinese back they found her impaled in the vertical position hands and legs tied behind her back on an ax handle driven into the ground. She died a very slow death because she gave aid to the south. They also left behind many mass execution

MASS EXECUTION SITE

sites killing all prisoners and anyone they thought sympathized with the south.

Bob said they did have some problems especially at night with "slicky boys", (thieves), infiltrators, and some sabotage, but the days were better. Cloudy nights were absolutely black because this part of the country did not have electric lights and blacked out villages were the norm because of the war. With no light to be reflected back from the clouds it was even difficult to see his own hands on moon-less nights.

Each night they set out five-gallon cans filled with sand which acted as a wick that when soaked with diesel fuel would burn all night. These cans were set far out in a

THIS OUTPOST WAS WELL HIDDEN FROM THE BOTTOM OF THE HILL BUT CONNECTED TO THE REST OF 62ND ENGINEER COMPANY WITH STEPS AND TRENCHES FACED WITH ROCK

perimeter around them, forming an outer circle of flaming light designed to prevent intrusion if possible. Barbed booby-trapped rolls of military constantina or razor wire and a barbed wire fence made up the next barrier in front of and overlooked by more lines of covered, camouflaged, and sandbagged trenches forming a second perimeter and a third even higher inner perimeter pocked with foxholes overlooked these. Each platoon was located on a different step or level going up the mountain. Levels were perhaps 50 to 100 foot above the last one. Stone steps were used to get up or down to trucks, water, supply area, etc. They were bunkered in the dark behind an earthen berm, so they could look out . . . but they could not be seen, with quick access to the trenches. Sentries caught off guard, could end up with a loop of piano wire around their necks. Once in position, the loop was jerked tight cutting the windpipe and stopping blood flow to the head. It was all done without a sound. Sentries were very careful!

While they worked during the day, they had well-armed sentries posted in the hills around them on watch. They were never far from their weapons.

One day hundreds of United Nation paratroopers dropped from planes, near and over the river valley. Several paratroopers ended up hanging from the bridges, or landed in the water and were dragged under and had to be rescued. It was difficult watching this interaction from our mountaintop advantage, watching their struggle and possible failure of some to survive.

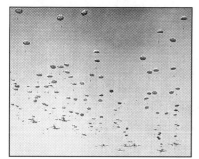

PARATROOPERS DROPPED FROM PLANES

November 7th, 1954, a RB-29 Photo reconnaissance plane was shot down by two communist MIGs killing one man with the other parachuting to safety.

Late 1954, The 62nd Engineer Combat Battalion would soon be ordered back to modernize Fort Leonard Wood, Mo. so Bob's group was transferred to Company C of the 84th Engineers Battalion and moved

PREPARING TO MOVE AND TEARING DOWN METAL BUILDINGS WE HAD JUST CONSTRUCTED FOR THE WINTER

down to an area that was an old destroyed Japanese Army Base and was to be rebuilt into a US Army military base. They were to tear down the quonsets they had just completed and rebuild them in Ascom City, (Army Support Command) near Inchon.

LOADING UP... LEAVING A BARE PATCH OF GROUND

Their old encampment was abandoned; all supplies, fuel, equipment, buildings and tents, were packed on trucks, and anything left behind was destroyed with phosphorus grenades and buried. Korean families were moving in even as they were leaving.

WORKING FROM DAWN TO DARK AND BEYOND GOT THEM INSIDE AS THE SNOW FELL AND WINTER SET IN

When they arrived in the Ascom City area they found devastation and a detachment of Marines already there so they set-up camp directly across the road from them. They constructed their new homes in numbing cold weather.

Also, soon after arriving Bob happened to meet and talk with **David Kranz** a classmate from Beaver Dam who getting ready to go home.

They now would spend the winter in nine man squad tents with wonderful wooden floors, two light bulbs, heated by two pot-type oil stoves set in sand-filled wooden boxes. They had canvass cots to sleep on, sleeping bags, and enclosed out-houses. They rebuilt their company orderly room, supply room, and mess hall using their old ones, and built a security fence with a gate and a guard tower.

With security in place, they hired orphan Korean children as houseboys to clean the tents, roll up sleeping bags, to take clothes to be washed in the village, and tend the fires. Their firearms were now stored in the supply room.

Bob was issued a case of bottled beer (covered by rusty metal caps) once in a while which was to be stored under his cot and cigarettes which he sold to a smoker.

Limited electric power and gas engine driven refrigerators soon arrived so food changed from combat rations to bulk ration mess-hall type food.

Somehow; slicky boys still were able to steal valuable equipment and newly hired civilian Korean workers would sneak out with salt, sugar, spices, clothing, etc. in small amounts hidden in their clothing. Food and basic needs stealing was more or less overlooked because the Koreans had so little for the deepening winter. Everyone worked very long hours to get the company compound ready for the winter of 1954 and 1955.

NEW SUPPLY ROOM AND 84TH ENGINEER'S COMPANY ORDERLY ROOM MADE FROM REUSED MATERIAL

Company 'C" hired 300 (KSC) Korean Service Corp thus creating jobs for civilians and also created a campground of military tents nearby where they could live. They were trained to help build roads, erect buildings, and to mix concrete. They also started working on a septic and lagoon system along with underground water and sewer utilities for the new Ascom City.

KOREAN SERVICE CORP (HOMELESS PEOPLE) HELPED TO BUILD THE NEW MILITARY POST

Supply ships brought in dozens of new straight side quonset kits so work crews poured concrete floor foundations for them and set them up at the rate of a dozen or more buildings each day. Bob headed a crew that surveyed, built and formed the foundations for each building and a second crew poured the concrete floors. The following day a third crew would setup the quonset, after which a forth crew customized the interior to fit the new occupant's needs and a last crew landscaped or cleaned up the area. The next week military units moved into these new buildings. There were several such crews working to build this new base. It fast became a large secure military base with more guard towers.

ROK SOLDIER TRAINEES

Two sometimes three (ROK) Republic of Korea soldiers were assigned to Bob every three months. He had to train them to be able take his place when he left their country so Bob taught his people to do carpenter work, squad leadership, and to speak English. He also learned a great deal of Korean. (Mostly terms to do with carpentry and construction materials)

A field hospital was to be relocated from the Seoul area of Korea to Ascom City, so engineers and the new Korean Service Corp people built; a water supply system, sewer connection, x-ray labs, operating rooms, fire stations, nurse's quarters, and electric power system for a new 121st Evacuation Hospital. It was there while working on the nurse housing building Bob suffered a broken jaw and teeth. A medic put his knee on Bob's chest and with a hammer and different type chisels, cut a hole into the bone of his upper jaw to remove broken roots of his teeth. It took at least 5 hours. The medic told Bob to get his teeth redone when he got back to the states. He would heal up fine! Conditions got better except they now had to salute officers and stand limited inspections. A Red Cross van would show up once a month, while they were working with warm hearted ladies serving hot coffee and real warm donuts!

RAMPS USED TO CONNECT WARDS TO OTHER PARTS OF THE HOSPITAL

RAMPS PROVIDED BUILDING SEPARATION IN CASE OF ATTACK AND FIRE

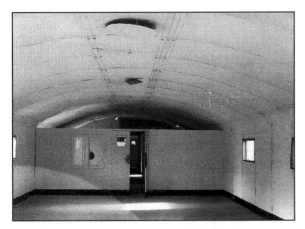

BEDS WOULD BE MOVED INTO THESE NEW WARDS

Bob was hanging the last doors in the new nurse quarters building when a nurse approached him. She had overheard he was going on R&R to Japan and asked him if he would bring her back some underwear. (the nurses hated military issue underwear) Note! This was the same nurse who a couple of days before had accused him of stealing her money from her room while he was hanging the door of her room. After her accusation, it dawned on her she had put her money in her bra that day at his request because he did not want to be responsible for any losses from her room. He was doing finishing touches to the building getting it ready for final new building inspection.

Bob was a squad leader (18 years old) during the Wolmi-Do riots. It was nasty, with thousands of civilian men, women, and children involved. His company trained for riot control and then moved to the site taking limited control with special crowd control formations and fixed

KITCHEN AND MESS HALL BUILDING

bayonets. Fear pushed the crowd back and he in turn was in fear as to what would happen if they didn't move back! It was not a fun time! A few days later, another outfit took over riot control with the added help of a water cannon flown in from Japan. It went on for months at different levels of concern. They were violently demonstrating against the United Nations truce thus ending most fighting before the reunification of Korea. South Korea is still formally at war with the North to this day!

Bob received two R&R (rest and recuperation) leaves to Japan while he was in Korea. The first one was by liberty ship (USS Sgt. Joseph Muller) to Kobe, Japan. (Major Naval Port)

They disembarked from the ship and just as they left the dock pimps pounced on them. Suddenly dozens of Military Police and Japanese Police staged a raid on the road in front of them, brutally throwing the pimps over their shoulders onto the brick road and arresting any they could catch. The

PORT AUTHORITY—KOBE

sound of flesh and bone smacking the brick was ghastly. The pimps not caught disappeared and no longer bothered them.

SHRINES OF KYOTO

He and his friends traveled to Kyoto which was about an hour away. Kyoto is the Paris of Japan. They spent 7 days relaxing and touring the area. It had beautiful historical sacred gardens and park areas enriched with beautiful shrines thus inspiring a very spiritual experience. He bashfully enjoyed the public baths in which entire Japanese families would frolic and

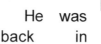

soak while nude. (Note! Everyone is required to take a cleansing pre-bath before they could enter the public baths.) (Soap was not allowed in the public bath area.) He also stopped at the Port Authority Post PX in Kobe as he was leaving Japan to pick some underwear for the nurse. He does not remember her size any more.

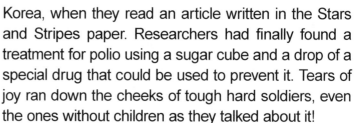

SACRED GARDENS

He was back in Korea, when they read an article written in the Stars and Stripes paper. Researchers had finally found a treatment for polio using a sugar cube and a drop of a special drug that could be used to prevent it. Tears of joy ran down the cheeks of tough hard soldiers, even the ones without children as they talked about it!

THE RECEIVING/REPLACEMENT DEPOT SERVED SOLDIERS ARRIVING IN KOREA OR LEAVING...
EQUIPPING THEM WITH CLOTHING, MEDICAL CHECKS, AND TRANSPORTATION

During the winter of 54-55, Bob was deeply involved in building a new Receiving/Replacement Troop Center, an Ordnance Depot, Motor Pool, many headquarters buildings, etc. for this Ascom City Military Post.

One of the more difficult problems they had to contend with was shortages of critical supplies. They were always short of certain foods, socks, sleeping bags, spark plugs, underclothes, and many other items, like plain old nails. There isn't even a word for nails in the Korea language. They were running jeeps on three cylinders and several vehicles were stripped of parts to keep others running.

IN ONE END AND OUT THE OTHER AND YOU WERE READY TO GO HOME OR LIVE IN KOREA

He decided to personally check out the food and clothing shortages and soon realized that, "supply truck run" people must be selling clothes and food on the Korean black market.

Bob had the occasion to stand inspection of the newly constructed troop replacement depot building by Colonel Peacock. (Battalion commander) After his inspection and approval of the building, Bob then asked him if he could speak off the record. It was granted! He then told Col. Peacock about the lack of clothes, food, etc. and how he discovered it might be going to the black market. Bob asked him to investigate. He thanked Bob for the information and said he would take care of it! The next afternoon a jeep and trailer pulled into their encampment loaded with clothing and sleeping bags. They were given socks, gloves, coats, and needed personal supplies directly off the trailer. They would at least be warm again and food in greater amounts was soon available instead of excuses. Moreover, after an investigation, two cooks, and two supply clerks were sentenced to the stockade. (military prison). Bob's name was never brought up in the court martial proceedings, but he almost got orders to take them to the stockade because it was on his military record that he did this type of detail at Fort Leonard Wood.

Christmas Eve night, 1954, Bob was to learn the meaning of terror and fear. He had guard duty and was posted near heavy equipment and fuel lines by a river when he was hit by unknown intruders. Passwords were not returned! Fear was so intense that panic engulfed him consuming his thoughts. His survival instincts took over as he scoured the night with his sight, smell, and hearing. Without giving his position away, he melded himself into his surroundings, took his rifle off safety and waited! The intruders upon hearing the click of his rifle being moved off safety must have been just as terrified and abruptly froze in place. They knew he was there but did not know where he was, so wisely just before dawn they slipped away! The equipment remained safe and secure.

February 5th, 1955, Red China & North Korea were threating to invade the islands of Matsu and Quemoy so the UN was conducting RB-45 photo reconnaissance missions off the coast of North Korea avoiding land by staying over the sea escorted by F-86 fighters to make sure North Korea was not doing a military build up to invade them. They ran into eight MIGs who opened fire on them. Our guys fired back shooting down two while chasing the other six back into communist territory. The marines located next to us went on full alert complete with field maneuvers.

Early spring 1955, Bob was transferred into the 44th Engineer Battalion. They now were blessed with metal barracks with steel bunk beds. Buildings included a day room and indoor latrine with showers.

They struggled with monsoon rains in the mountains sometimes working one to three days without sleep at critical times reconstructing roads, sandbagging washouts, repairing air strips, etc.

For the first time they spread oil on certain dirt roads and started blacktopping some important roads. Poppa-san with his water buffalo and cart frequently would cut across and make a mess out of freshly laid road in spite of previous day warnings to wait until it cured. They also built additional military buildings, supply depots, and started constructing ship locks in the Inchon harbor area. The project included blasting the top of a mountain off and moving it into the sea to make a huge lock system so ships could stay docked while the 20-30 foot plus tide moved in and out. It was not yet complete when Bob left Korea.

There was a time (**June 1955**) when a North Korean pilot defected and flew in under the radar with a YAK-18 plane. The U.S. and U.N. sought to investigate its technology and build counter measures against it. It did however shake up the military because it made it in without detection until it landed. It landed on a runway in a nearby air base just as two of our planes were taking off causing quite a surprise as scuttle butt had it! Embarrassed brass (commanding officers) quickly responded by ordering a

YAK-18 PLANE UNDER GUARD

lot of AAA gunner training with drone planes towing air targets high over the seacoast. Jets started patrolling the sky more carefully, the marines stationed near them did extra maneuvers, security was tightened up, and brass did lots of combat readiness inspections, but eventually nerves quieted down.

One day Bob and a friend were walking on the road killing time when a jeep with a flag and star drove by unnoticed. It was a General! His driver backed the jeep up, so the General could confront them. He demanded to know why they did not salute his vehicle. They were honest and told him they had not noticed his vehicle. Suddenly he changed his tone of voice and ordered them to get into to his jeep. They were in deep trouble! After checking to see if they had duty for the afternoon, he took them to see a USO show at a nearby airfield hanger starring Debbie Reynolds. Now that was a surprise and they even had front area seats! They had to find our own way back after the show.

One of the more unusual things that happened to him in Korea took place at night. Someone sabotaged the fuel lines running above ground next to and along the shoreline of the river to a fuel dump base many miles inland. The broken line spilled fuel into the river as the water flowed back toward the sea. Suddenly, a fire broke out far inland causing riverside buildings located along the river to burst into flame! Bob and his companions were on high ground north of Inchon near the sea and could see this gigantic, rolling, spreading, silent explosion, hurtling toward them on the river. Bob knew it was causing devastation, loss of homes and perhaps lives and will remember that sight the rest of his life!

On Bob's second R&R, he flew with perhaps 30 other soldiers and two friends to Tokyo, Japan in a cavernous double deck military troop plane which was returning to Japan after making a delivery of heavy equipment. The upper deck was in a folded position so they sat in nylon strap seats hung on the walls. It was very noisy and cold with heavy frost covering the plane's metal walls.

He and his friends rode the train along the coast to Yokohama and back enjoying the land, mountains, and people. They hired Japanese ladies to guide and to share Japanese culture with them. These ladies were companions, not prostitutes. The ladies spoke broken English and nicely guided them through historic parts of the city and through the markets helping them buy gifts and silk goods at fair prices, which Bob and his two friends shipped back to family in the states.

Japan was still far from being rebuilt from WW II. Thousands of buildings and most every city were still in some state of ruin! Then . . . back to Korea . . .

Sept. 1955, he transferred to the motor pool as he wanted to see as much of Korea as possible before he left that part of the world. He drove a jeep for about two months and got the chance to see many U.S. installations and much of South Korea.

Oct. 1955, he bought a bottle of Corbin Whiskey and he and his friends finished it. He put the yellow ribbon on his shirt and enjoyed being a short-timer with its special privileges. No more dangerous duty and no more inspections!

Bob (now driving a jeep) was involved with a different reconstruction project one day. The men were repairing and rebuilding one of many burned out buildings damaged from bombs and shells. Suddenly, a long high multi-story stone

BURNED OUT WALLS

and mortar wall toppled over crushing or killing several of his friends and several Korean Service Corp. Men had their feet crushed flat, heel to toe, as they tried to escape and several people were maimed for life! They had to dig them out, get the living medical help, and get the dead into body bags. Had he not transferred just a couple of weeks before, he might have been one of them. He will always remember that day, also!

One night they had a near riot. Some black, Cuban, and white soldiers got stinking drunk and were spoiling for a fight. Perhaps 40 to 50 men broke the bases off liquor bottles (using the neck as a handle with the jagged glass base protruding from it) and still others had knifes. It was static all high pitched bluster and threats when someone fired a burst of semi-automatic rifle fire overhead through the steel building walls. The rattling bullets brought everything to a halt in a hurry with everyone embracing the floor! They never found out who did the shooting.

November, 1955, Bob got his orders to go home. He turned in his equipment, rifle, and combat area clothes at the same Reception/Replacement Center he and his friends had helped to build. Note! When soldiers leave Korea you go in one door; turn in all your equipment, strip and turn in your clothes, delouse, shower, medical check, get new clothes, stuff your personal and new stuff into a duffle bag, and leave a transformed person at a different door on the

CATTLE TRUCK RIDE

TAXI RIDE ARRIVING TO TAKE US OUT TO THE SHIP

other end. You might enjoy a nice cold November ride (as he did) in an open air cattle truck to the Inchon coast, leave Korea in a madly twisting and bouncing landing craft and then with a full duffle bag struggle up a rope cargo net swinging over the side of a tilting and swaying troop ship a mile or two out in the Bay of Inchon and joyfully sail down the Yellow Sea, touch the East China Sea, cross the Korean Straits, cross the Sea of Japan and sail up the Pacific for Yokohama, Japan.

Bob was part of a Christmas shipment of 250 pleasantly surprised troops that transferred off the troop ship USS Randall in Yokohama, Japan to an aircraft carrier (USS Windham Bay) headed for the U.S.A. They sailed across the Pacific directly into a violent three day storm near Hawaii which threatened to break up the carrier. Air Crews and sailors moved the planes off the flight deck and tied down planes and

ENJOYING THE DECK OF THE USS WINDHAM BAY

equipment. No one was allowed on deck except sailors on watch and even they had safety ropes attached. During the storm, the massive sidewalls of the carrier would split open or steel wall beams and posts would break loose. Running sailors would slap splices of steel on them and quickly weld them. (Electric welders hung on the walls about 30 feet apart) Each time a huge wave would suspend the ship by its middle, or the ship was caught suspended between two huge waves, there would be this tremendous groan and then the snapping of steel and again men would rush to repair another part of the ship. It was frightening to see outside light coming through some of the new cracks and open joints in the outside walls of the plane storage deck located below the flight deck. It really did unnerve Bob! Many people including sailors and air crews were sea-sick! Finally, it was over!

There was plenty of space on the carrier and great food. (real ice cream!) They weren't required to work or do (watch) guard duty! The sailors and air crews couldn't do enough for them and treated them with awesome respect making them feel really special.

Those on board from Korea were given special shots and drugs to protect them against leprosy, encephalitis, etc. and Bob was told not to donate blood for at least seven years after he arrived home.

Twenty-three days after they left Korea, they sailed under the San Francisco bridge. Choking back tears 250 happy men stood on deck beaming as they were coming home to

THE GOLDEN GATE BRIDGE USA

NAVAL BASE - SAN FRANCISCO - AIR CRAFT CARRIERS

America! They docked near three huge aircraft carriers and were welcomed with navy band music. They boarded a bus to a local base where Bob got a haircut and orders to fly to Chicago.

Bob got his release papers near Chicago at Great Lakes Military Base and hopped on a bus to Beaver Dam. He would be home for Christmas!

After returning home to Beaver Dam, he had to spend six more years in the Ready Reserves requiring him to be ready to go back to active duty upon 24-hour notice.

Formosa, now called Taiwan, was in danger of invasion by Communist China. He

REBUILT KOREAN HOME WITH FAMILY

received two, get ready to go notices, but never got, "the go order". The Chinese mainland would back-off each time after threatening to invade the islands. He was very happy about that! Eventually, he would receive an honorable discharge.

The following story (sent to the author by someone unknown) describes the quality of life, duty, and physical conditions that U.S. Armed Forces lived in and worked under during cease-fire deployment in defense of the demilitarized zone. It is from the perspective of a Military Policeman, but most conditions apply to all units serving in Korea. These conditions were similar to actual combat conditions; the harshness, the long period of time, and very tense and uncertain circumstances, caused considerable fighting among unit members, between units, and with Korean nationals. These conditions caused frequent AWOLs and desertions, and caused many good soldiers to break with regulation and end up being Court Martialed and serving stockade time.

1955, their Military Police Company arrival was by troop ship through Inchon. After exiting the landing craft, reporting one's self present and loading on to open trucks, (cattle trucks) troops were moved to the Receiving Center. Class A uniforms were turned in upon arrival in the country and were not returned until your tour of duty was completed. There were no "civvies" to wear and were not authorized. Fatigues were the combat, duty, and dress uniform of the day.

All tours in Korea were a minimum of sixteen (16) months continuous service. This deployment was considered a "hardship tour" by the military. Sixteen months is an excessive amount of time to endure the conditions that follow. This is in comparison to the six (6) months rotational deployments of today's operations under similar conditions.

Alerts required full combat gear and basic ammo loads. You took up defensive positions either within your own compound or moved to divisional positions.

Civilian Checkpoints and Traffic Control Points existed for civilians on all military service roads. Koreans were required to have special identification and authorization for foot and vehicle movement within, or into or out of, the division area. All vehicles were quick searched. Military personal (U.S. and Allied) were also required to produce identification and a military vehicle trip-ticket to pass. Security was tight.

Smudge pots were lit for protection around the compound perimeters at night to increase visibility and the detection of infiltrators, North Korean sympathizers, or slicky-boys (local thieves). These hits were frequent.

Communication with Koreans was strictly forbidden, except with Korean soldiers assigned to U.S. units and Korean civilians hired to do work in the compounds while in the compound. This offense was subject to Court Martial. There could be no stopping or stepping off the Military Service Road while in transit from one compound to another by any U.S. Military personnel. This offense was subject to Court Martial.

Water was very scarce, and you full body washed, washed your hair, and shaved with the same water using your helmet or a pan as a container. If the mess hall was willing to give you warm water, you had to carry it back to your tent. This was seldom.

Showers were available once a week or so if the water point had enough. Water shortages were frequent. The shower water was not always warm. There was no hot or cold water for washing during spring or summer because there was no heating facility in the tent. You brushed your teeth with canteen water. General dental health was close to non-existent. This person never had a dental checkup in sixteen months.

There were no night clubs, post exchanges, service clubs, snack bars, movie theaters, or other places to go when off duty. Occasionally 3.2 beer could be had in the mess tent. A service center was later built in 1956 with a quonset hut movie theater and snack bar. It served the whole division and soldiers had to be trucked in by unit. Passes were granted under special conditions to visit relatives or friends located in other units within your division area. You had to prove that transport to and from the visiting area would be available. There was no female companionship for 16 months except when on (R&R) Rest and Recuperation leave to Japan. There were no telephone calls home or anywhere else except in family life/death emergencies and there was no guarantee that there would be a mail call. There were no gifts to purchase and send home unless bought while on R&R or by friend on R&R. For a sixteen month tour, two 7 day R&Rs were authorized and Japan was the only R&R option. Huge responsibilities created an under strength condition, resulting in one R&R at best. The MP Company had the main traffic platoons at MP Headquarters with detachments for the DMZ and Division Headquarters. Many soldiers rotated to the detachments or to MP Headquarters and lost their place in the R&R rotation order. Normal leave time didn't apply to this tour.

There were occasional visits by the Salvation Army or Red Cross with doughnuts, cigarettes, toilet paper and chewing gum.

Daily duty, during 1955, frequently involved as much as eighteen hours of continuous duty. This included regular duty, perimeter guard, unexpected patrols and details to assist on-duty personnel, emergency details (tent fires, mud slides, icing conditions, etc.), digging area defensive positions, drainage ditches, and latrines, building permanent retaining walls and constructing board sidewalks for the rainy season, building or repairing other facilities, special transport and escort duties, vehicle wash point detail, and other incidental duties as they arose. It was not unusual to begin perimeter guard at 2400 hours, come off perimeter guard at 0600 hours, eat, dig trenches for two hours, wash jeeps, clean weapons, prepare for duty, report for patrol duty briefing and guard mount at 1500 hours and end patrol duty at 2345 hours.

There were incidents at the Demilitarized Zone, infiltrators were caught, and North Korean and Chinese harassment was common including rounds fired across the line, flares illuminating the DMZ, horns and bugles blaring, propaganda loudspeakers and flood lights. The DMZ fences were lower and easier to cross. Military Policemen, Recon Co. and Infantry vehicle patrols, rode in the winter with jeep tops down. These patrols always had a third man in the gun ring with a 50 cal. machinegun. Temperatures often got to 15 degrees below with steady 35 mph winds blowing from the north. Seat positions had to rotate often to warm faces because faces would get so cold you could not move your mouth to speak.

Living areas were leaky eight man squad tents. In the winter they were heated with pot belly stoves and No. 2 oil and frequently caught fire. During the spring and summer the tents leaked and were bug infested. All toilet facilities were outdoors and were open tubes stuck in the ground, exposed to everyone, or an outhouse with a bench seat and two cutout holes, and no heat. You froze in winter often with hard yellow ice on the seats, and in the wet spring it swarmed with insects and flying bugs. In the summer you gagged! Toilet paper was gold!

Electricity was sometimes available in some rear areas.

There were no paved roads above Seoul so all military service roads were narrow and many were rutty. You were covered in dust when it was dry and mud when it rained. Driving was very difficult and treacherous in many areas. God smiled upon us, but the Defense Department had the last word. (Unknown)

Late March of 1955, **Douglas Randall** arrived in Korea. His assignment was to the United Nations Command, Military Armistice Joint Security Force. Their headquarters was at Munsan-ni, but he was located at Advance Camp at Panmunjom. One platoon remained at Munsan-ni to provide security of the headquarters area. The remainder of the unit was at Advance Camp with the following duties:

1. Security posts at the Panmunjom conference area,
2. Security at Advance Camp.
3. Escort of Neutral Nations personnel throughout South Korea (included air and surface travel) (armed officer personnel only.)

NORTH KOREAN GUARDS

The security posts in the conference area were all walking patrols jointly with North Korean security guards. With the exception of a few incidents of personal harassment, we had no problems walking security posts with our enemies. The escorts of the neutral nations personnel representing the Allies (Swiss and Swedes) were routine except that they were the only unit in Korea at that time that was authorized sedans. Escorting the neutral nations personnel representing the Communists was more complicated. All the movements of their personnel had to be done by aircraft with blacked out windows so that the Czechs and Poles would not be able to observe our military installations and report them to the North Koreans. The truce was still very fragile at that time.

PANMUNJOM CONFERENCE AREA

CLOTHING DISCARDED BY COMMUNIST POWS

ADVANCE CAMP

The road from Munsan-ni to Advance Camp was very interesting also, at least to Doug as a first time arrival to Korea. This road went across Freedom Gate Bridge over the Imjin River which had been very much in the news as part of the route of Operation Big and Little Switch prisoner of war exchanges. Freedom Gate Bridge itself had explosives in place so that in case the North Koreans would again attack to the south, the bridge could be blown. All along the road, the ditches were strewn with clothing that had been discarded by prisoners as they were moving to the exchange points. Along the road also were entrenchments and defensive positions left from the war. Advance Camp was located on the southern edge of the demilitarized zone, so there were no military troops north of them. There were no Korean civilian personnel permitted north of the Imjin River, except those employed by US Forces. The area around Advance Camp was never cleared of mines, so it was not unusual for land mines to spontaneously explode in what had been rice paddies. Presumably, the mines went off because of some wild animals tripping them or simple degrading of the mines due to exposure to the weather. Douglas was transferred to Tokyo, Japan in November 1955.

Late 1956, **Don Laabs** of Beaver Dam landed at Inchon. He would work in an engineer supply depot receiving and checking out lumber, nails, and other supplies.

Eventually he transferred to the 1st Cav located about 40 miles north of Seoul. While there a call came down for a volunteer to be an observer to the talks at Panmunjom. Don volunteered and after a short introduction on protocol he donned an arm band and clearance badge and was taken by truck to a building set exactly on center on the 38th parallel. The conference table was also centered on this line. He found it interesting for each person to speak and then interpreters would do their part so everyone understood.

THE CONFERENCE TABLE

He recalls passing a Turkish encampment and was startled to see two dead men hanging on the gate posts. It was a visual warning to any North Korean infiltrators. He returned to the states in 1958 on a "General" ship encountering a 3 day typhoon on the way. He recalls that everyone was sick including ship personal. Upon returning home he joined the reserves training each summer and one weekend a month.

December 1956, **Eugene Hintz** tells the story of a short-timers swagger stick. It was typically given to individuals of a unit when they were considered a short-timer with 30 days left until their rotation back to the United States. This brass stick was made from a 105mm artillery shell powder train (this was the mechanism containing a type of powder in the middle of the shell to make all of the explosive powder ignite at one time), with the ends capped with a 50 caliber machine gun casing and tip all welded together. During the final 30 days of a tour, a short-timer was not given any extra duty and was also saluted by the officers of the unit instead of having to salute them which is common military courtesy, and allowed to go to the head of any line, such as for meals or drawing equipment at the supply room.

When you arrived at the point of thirty days left in Korea, you were expected to drink a 5th of Corbin's whiskey with the help of buddies. This completed, the little yellow ribbon was removed from the bottle and pinned to your shirt lapel. This meant you had thirty days left, don't mess with me!

February 1967, Douglas Randall was assigned back to the Republic of Korea again. On arrival, he was assigned as Deputy Provost Marshal of the Second Infantry Division, until the departure of the incumbent Provost Marshal, when he would take his place. While in the 2nd Division, he was promoted to Lieutenant Colonel. The normal tour in Korea at that time was now twelve months, but he was extended for about six weeks until his replacement arrived.

USS PUEBLO

Jan. 23, 1968 His tour time in Korea included capture of the USS Pueblo, a U.S. Navy intelligence ship, by North Korea off its coast. The North Koreans also sent an assassination squad south to assassinate the South Korean president. Fortunately, they were intercepted before they got to Seoul.

The Home Front . . . 1951, during the Korean War, Olin Industries was awarded the contract to manage Badger Ordinance (powder plant) near Baraboo, Wisconsin. In order to get the Badger Plant into operational shape, Olin replaced machinery, office furniture, critical supplies, and added building production areas such as the ball powder plant. At that time, Olin Industries was the only manufacturer of ball powder in the United States. Ball powder is a fine-grained, spherical gun powder coated in graphite that is easy to store and transport in any climate and ideal for modern infantry small arms ammunition cartridges. The time it took to build the ball powder plant at Badger was too long to enable any of the ball powder produced there to be used in the Korean War so it was put into storage and eventually used during the Vietnam War. This plant however did produce: acid, oleum, smokeless powder, and rocket propellant for the Korean War. Many people from Beaver Dam worked in this plant.

1952, **Monarch Range** of Beaver Dam acquired land and built a shell plant for the Korean War. They produced shells at an enormous rate reaching one million shells. Then local union members decided to go on strike forcing the government to remove shell equipment and gave it to another contract manufacturer. In Korea munitions were so short desperate soldiers and civilians walked in mine fields to gather shell casings so ordinance could reuse them.

BEAVER DAM PRODUCED 1,000.000
BY JUNE, 1953 FOR THE KOREAN WAR

DEAD, WOUNDED, MISSING

JUNE 25, 1950 THROUGH JANUARY 31, 1955—OFFICIAL PERIOD OF THE KOREAN POLICE ACTION.

- 36,913 documented deaths in Korea and surrounding waters (both hostile 33,651 and Non-hostile 3,262)
- Hostile deaths include 8,177 a mix of KIA, MIA and POW.
- 103,284 surviving hospitalized wounded in action in Korea, undoubtedly there were a number of hospitalized WIA cases that did not get recorded; no records were kept for non-hospitalized wounded.
- 131 Wounded in action in the DMZ insofar as it is known.

The rogue nation of North Korea is ruled by paranoid cult-like dictators. Paranoia would drive them to burrow underground and to close the country to outsiders. The fear of air power drove them and whole parts of their society deep underground. Not only had they dug invasion tunnels to the south under the DMZ many times, but whole sections of their society moved underground and now spend their entire lives underground carving out and setting up a hidden complex for atom bomb development, massive military establishments, whole cities, manufacturing, schools, and critical storage.

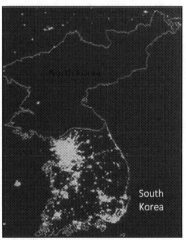

SATELLITE PICTURE OF KOREA
FROM SPACE
NOTE! THE DIFFERENCE OF NIGHT
LIGHTS BETWEEN NORTH AND
SOUTH KOREA

The young people of North Korea sign up to serve their god-like father figure dictators and move underground to excavate these complexes and for the rest of their lives are rewarded with better income, food, and cult prestige. After 5 to 8 years of work they earn the right to marry someone else who lives underground and to have a family. Escapees from North Korea, speak of tunnel highways and railroads connecting these underground establishments. North Korea has been effectually tunneling and excavating underground for over 50 years to the point that satellite pictures show only limited night lighting above ground as compared with the South Korea.

As very small children they are indoctrinated to believe their sacred leaders provide them with everything good while any shortcomings are blamed on outsiders. All sources of information are tightly controlled so this closed society is cheated of all forms of freedom that outside knowledge brings.

North Korean Leaders have now formally cancelled the truce of 1953 and continue to provoke the south with small scale attacks killing or injuring many people each year. This counterfeit peace lies molten ready to reach out to set the world on fire! The "Forgotten War" will eventually bite us once again!

The race into space

SPUTNIK

Oct 4th 1957 came the dawn of the space race. Busy Beaver Dam workers in the shoe factory, in food processing plants, grocery stores, farmers, etc. heard the news mostly by word of mouth. They were stunned and somewhat humiliated that the U.S.S.R. (Soviet Union) a communist country had proudly placed Sputnik into the sky over the U.S. and the world. Communist countries fought us to a stand-still in Korea and now they were smugly moving ahead of us in space exploration and arming themselves with sophisticated and supersize offensive weapons. This energized the humbled leadership of the United States to set-up a new civilian National Aeronautics and Space Agency (NASA) program with the goal to catch up and surpass the Soviet Union in space.

SPACE SHUTTLE LIFT OFF AT SPACE CENTER

KENNY SPACE CENTER

WALKING ON THE MOON

The Cold War/Counterfeit Peace period included an arms race

TITAN MISSILE SILO

U-2 SPY PLANE

AIRCRAFT

This also rattled the military research establishment of this country. Our military burrowed into mountains with control centers and thrust missile silos into the ground. Water and sky were now highways for military options. Soon nuclear tipped rockets set in silos were spreading across this world and the futile arms race was on.

AIR DEFENSE MISSILES

A network of spy planes and counter intelligence agents flooded the world keeping an eye on the other superpower

The "Cold War" was fought in many ways. **Gene Norenberg of Beaver Dam** did his part in his own quiet way. His work was "top secret". Only now does he speak a little of his work. He also told me part of his work included transporting fuel to nuclear missile sites. I used declassified public domain pictures to illustrate the type of areas where he did his work.

NUCLEAR BOMB TESTS

(RADAR BLIND) DELTA WING

NUCLEAR CARRIERS

43

He spent much of his time located on an air force base. This picture depicts a typical base, with the all-important hangers and planes. Missile silos would located in ever-greater circles around this base.

TYPICAL AIR FORCE BASE WITH MISSILE INSTALLATION

NUCLEAR SUBMARINES

X-15

BATH TUB

XB TEST PLANE

"This was called the bathtub". It was released from the wing of a B-52. It was built to do the same as the X-15, but never worked well. Crashed a lot!

The X-15 was built to fly to the edge of outer space. (Used to evaluate future astronauts) It was released from the wing of a B52. It was part of his (Gene's) job to fill it with liquid oxygen

The United States made great strides moving ahead with land, sea, sky and space programs. Eventually the Soviet Union would collapse,
   but in the mean-time . . .

SOUTH AMERICA—POVERTY

The United States was very concerned that many parts of South America would succumb to communist influence. The poor in these countries had nothing but despair for their futures. Poor people with nothing are easily swayed to turn on their country's leaders.

It was the mission of Americans like Doug Randall and others to evaluate and address this poverty problem and to channel American aid and funds effectively to combat poverty and thus communist influence. This aid was to give these people a new source of better living other than dependence on drug production for war lords.

DOUGLAS RANDALL was assigned to a Civil Affairs Detachment activated to be employed during the Cold War against the Communist backed insurgencies in emerging countries in South and Central America, Africa, southeast Asia and the Middle East. The members of the new Civil Affairs Detachment all attended a short course in counter insurgency at the Civil Affairs and Military Government School at Fort Gordon. After that short course of about four weeks, they were placed on temporary duty with the Special Warfare School at Fort Bragg, N.C. The school there was an orientation on Special Forces operations, counter insurgency and the group he was assigned to all received a brief course in conversational Spanish.

They were then assigned to the 3rd Civil Affairs Detachment and attached to the 8th Special Forces Group on orders to the Panama Canal Zone. Although not Special Forces qualified, they were all required to wear the Special Forces insignia and the green beret.

Upon arrival in Panama, they were stationed at Fort Gulick on the Atlantic side of the isthmus. Their first task was to learn more Spanish, however before he finished the initial training course, he was sent to Costa Rica as part of a

PANAMA CANAL ZONE

team to assess the threat of a communist insurgency in that country. Costa Rica is unique among Latin American countries in that a majority of the population speaks some English, is very proud of it and eager to practice it with North Americans. It was only a two week stay in Costa Rica which included travels throughout most of the country. Costa Rica had no army, so they had to conduct their survey as it pertained to the Guardia Civile (national police force).

Upon his return to Panama, he was placed into an extended Spanish language course which was intended to cover the same material that is taught in the six month course in the Army Language School, but they were to cover it in three months. At the completion of the course, most of them were tested and certified as being bilingual.

After that course, he was selected as part of a team to go to Bolivia for six months. His specific assignment was to manage a colonization project in the eastern portion of Bolivia in an area that was very close to the Amazon River Valley. Although he was assigned to Civil Affairs as the staff Public Safety Officer (law enforcement), he had majored in the biological aspects of conservation in college, therefore, he was selected to activate a unit in the Bolivian army to function similar to the Civilian Conservation Corps in the US during the depression. At that time, the average annual income of an agricultural family living in the Andes was about $100. The theory was to prepare a colonization site in the virgin jungle areas of eastern Bolivia after which selected families would be moved from the rocky mountainous area to the colonization area.

CLEARING THE JUNGLE—BUILDING HOUSING

The first work on the project site was to clear jungle vegetation to permit construction of a basic tropical house using native materials, then clear a garden patch and plant the first crop of a subsistence garden, then a family would be moved to the site about the time the garden crop was ready. This was to be done for fifty family plots of one hectare (2 1/2 acres) each. The US agency responsible for the project was the Agency for International Development (USAID) located in the ambassadors office. AID would administer and finance the project but did not have the personnel to provide on the job supervision. That was Doug's job.

TERRITORIAL LAND COMPANY

BULLDOZER SCHOOL

When he arrived in Bolivia, he found that nothing was ready to go. None of the equipment had even been ordered and personnel to staff the unit to be called the Territorial Land Company (TLC) had not even been recruited into the Army. After ordering all the equipment necessary, there was nothing for him to do until the equipment arrived, was checked, and the personnel were available to go to work. For that interim time, he was temporarily assigned to a bulldozer operation school in Cochabomba. There were three US engineer sergeants as part of our team that would instruct Bolivian soldiers to operate three D-7 bulldozers provided by USAID. He spent about six weeks on that project in which he was responsible for the administration and finance of the school.

When the equipment started arriving, he returned to La Paz to receive and store the equipment until the personnel for the Territorial Land Company arrived, were uniformed, and ready to move to the work site. At the time, Bolivia was experiencing an extremely high unemployment rate, as a result, when the recruitment notice was publicized, there were ten times as many applicants as they had a need for. Some of the applicants had never owned a pair of factory made shoes before. Because most of them were from the vicinity of the capitol city, La Paz, which is at 12,000 ft. elevation, none of them were familiar with thick forests, mosquitoes, and other insects nor how to use basic tools, such as machete and axe. They were also accustomed to the thin, dry air of the higher elevation and had to undergo a period of acclimatization to the heat and humidity of the Amazon River Valley. Since they were not used to the presence of insects, they were not aware that by scratching insect bites, they could cause an infection. At one time we had forty percent of the unit incapacitated from infections of one type or the other.

ROAD TO THE WORK SITE

The work site was located about one hundred miles from La Paz, which was a journey of about 10 to 12 hours depending on road conditions. During the rainy season, it was impossible to make the trip even with four wheel drive vehicles. Eventually, with the help of a Bolivian Army Engineer battalion, the roads were improved enough that a three quarter ton truck with four wheel drive and a winch could make the trip in the rainy season. Despite all the difficulties, at the end of six months, significant progress had been made so that he could turn the project over to his Bolivian counterpart. He did return a month later for a short time to assist in transferring the project completely to the Bolivian Army.

When he returned to Panama, the Third Civil Affairs Detachment had been transferred out of the Special Forces and attached directly to Southern Command Headquarters. The Detachment had also been physically moved to Fort Clayton on the Pacific side of the isthmus. The primary mission of the

PANAMA CANAL PROTECTION

Detachment was to teach the Latin American armed forces to conduct civic action in their own country. Civic Action meant to use the resources and talents of the military to assist the civilian populace and to contribute to the development of the country.

WORKSITE OF TERRITORIAL LAND COMPANY

He had a period of duty in the Canal Zone during the anti-American riots in Panama City in 1964. He also assisted with preparation of the civil defense plan for the Canal Zone Government as well as the US military installations in Panama. The entire Civic Action (CA) Detachment also spent a period of time assisting in the preparation of emergency plans for the entire Latin American region.

In between other assignments, he went to the Republic of Paraguay as part of a team to assess the threat of Communism there, and to recommend areas where the armed forces might be able to implement civic action.

He also went on a short trip to Costa Rica to assess the damage from the eruption of a dry volcano, Mt. Irazu and recommend actions by the Guardia Civile to assist.

On completion of the trip to Costa Rica, he was part of a team to the Central American country of El Salvador to establish medical or first aid clinics in remote areas of the country where medical resources were not available. The medical personnel were to conduct some immunizations of local people and to help the Salvadoran armed forces to provide medically trained personnel to operate the clinics. The team was intended to remain in El Salvador for six months to insure that the project was activated and in progress. However, after only about two weeks of operation, the capitol city was struck by a major

EMERGENCY HOUSING

earthquake resulting in more than a hundred deaths and hundreds of homes devastated. The mission of the team was immediately changed to one of disaster relief. In coordination with the US ambassadors office, the Salvadoran government and armed forces, it was determined that temporary homes would be built. The Salvadoran armed forces would provide an engineer battalion

U.S. PROVIDED EMERGENCY SHELTERS

to perform the construction, the US State Department would provide disaster relief funds, and the Salvadoran government would make real estate available and in conjunction with welfare agencies provide temporary tent shelter until the project was completed. He and an engineer major from US forces in Panama would be responsible for the implementation and supervision of the project. They would also be responsible for all the expenditure of US relief funds.

EUROPE (as adapted from State Department Records)

June 24th 1948, the blockade of Berlin to the West begins. The Berlin problem was the result of bad planning and paranoia. Berlin was also a divided city in a divided country and was the result of the failure of the East and West to agree on German unification. Berlin was caught in a recurring cycle of crisis and resolution, pitting in opposition the legality of Western Allies rights against the reality of Soviet Union military power.

June 25th 1948, the West begins the Berlin airlift of food and supplies when the Soviet Union pursued

CANDY FOR THE CHILDREN DROPPED BY AIR DURING THE FOOD AIRLIFT

FOOD FOR BERLIN

a land blockade of Berlin to protest Western efforts to integrate their zones of occupation in Western Germany. By restricting access to the city, the Soviets hoped to force the Western Allies to abandon a recently undertaken currency reform and possibly Berlin itself. The United States and its allies responded with a massive airlift that delivered supplies to the people of Berlin and generated overwhelming popular support in return. By the time the blockade was lifted in May 1949, the Allies had established not only the Federal Republic of Germany (West Germany) but also the North Atlantic Treaty Organization (NATO). The Soviets had suffered a major set-back.

In March of 1951, **DONALD R. JACOB** enlisted in the U.S. Air Force and went to Lackland Air Force Base, San Antonio, Texas for basic training. Classes were taught on Air Force regulations, history and math. They also had a class in chemical warfare which included; putting on a mask and clearing it in a room where a tear gas bomb was set off. They then had to leave the building slowly and orderly while eyes were burning. Fun-fun-fun. They also had instruction in small arms and had a day on the firing range. Marching and drilling was always a fun thing to do, especially in the Texas sun. There were also the memorable lectures and movies on communicable diseases.

After basic training, he was sent to Fort Francis E. Warren, Cheyenne, Wyoming. They flew out of San Antonio on a DC3 charter flight but soon landed in Lubbock, Texas for two-hour layover because of bad weather. After taking off again, bad weather again forced them to return to Lubbock, TX for an hour. When they finally got going again they flew by way of New Mexico and then on up to Cheyenne, Wyo. The flight was so rough that most of the people were sick including the flight attendant.

Note! Fort Frances E Warren later became a Strategic Air Command (SAC) base but at this time it was a training base with several different military schools. Don was assigned to the clerk typist school. His schooling consisted of orderly room procedures; including typing, making out morning reports, etc. This was a twelve-week course.

Cheyenne was a sleepy western cow town back in 1951. Frontier Days was in progress so he got to see his first rodeo. It was also the first time he saw hail as big as soft balls. He connected with RAY ALBRECHT, his neighbor from Beaver Dam, who was stationed there. Ray and his wife took him on a tour of some of the ranches and up into the mountains.

In August, he was sent to Scott Air Force Base outside of Bellville, Illinois for twelve more weeks of schooling for Cryptography training. Cryptography is encoding and decoding classified messages. Here he learned how to use and operate the different types of encoding equipment. Schooling was difficult as there was no way of taking any homework home because of security reasons. Everything had to be learned in the classroom and everyone had to have a security check done on them. After Don was discharged and returned home, his neighbors informed him the FBI had been around asking questions about him.

At Scott Air Force Base, Don did get to see Harry James and his orchestra. St. Louis was not too far away and it was a great place with a lot of good Dixie Land bands. The old St. Louis Browns (baseball) team invited the military to their games for free, but Don speculates it was because no one else would attend to them.

After finishing school he had a 15-day furlough in December of 1951 before reporting to Camp Kilmer, New Jersey for shipping out to Germany. Christmas and New Year's Eve was spent at Camp Kilmer. The new year came in with Don stuck with pulling midnight (KP) kitchen police duty. He was a big hit when he gave everyone left over sweet potatoes from Christmas, whether they wanted it or not.

On New Year's Day, they boarded a bus for Westover Air Force Base in Massachusetts where they took an overnight flight to Rhine Main AF Base, Frankfort, Germany.

Their plane developed engine problems on the way forcing them to land in the Azores. They were warmly dressed in their winter "blues" but found the temperature on the island was in the upper eighties.

Upon landing at Rhien Main Air Base, he was bused to 12th Air Force Headquarters at Wiesbaden, Germany for further assignment.

Don was assigned to 1946 AACS Squadron, Berlin, Germany. The Crypto Center was in a room without windows, and a double locked door common to all the centers he in which worked. His job involved security communication and filing all reports pertaining to communications. They also had to start the paper work on any new airmen on the base requiring a security classification.

On September 13, 1953, he had the misfortune of being hit by a car in front of the base while crossing the street and spent the next five months in various hospitals in Berlin and Wiesbaden with a broken leg.

Don was in the hospital at Christmas time so he got to play Santa Claus with the help of the Red Cross. He was dressed in a Santa outfit and his sleigh was a wheel chair from which he passed out gifts provided by the Red Cross for everyone in the hospital.

In 1943, while his brother was in the army, he had been hit by a car and spent time in the hospital. Eleven years later, Don did the same thing. Luckily, they were the only injuries either of them received.

Although he was in during the Korean War era, at no time was he in a combat zone. The only terse time came on June 16, 1953 when the German people in Berlin revolted against the Russians and were throwing rocks at the Russians and their tanks. They were a 109 miles behind the Iron Curtain in Berlin so there was a bit of concern and while most bases had a document destruction plan and an evacuation plane in case of emergency they had only a destruction plan.

The joke for new men to be stationed in Berlin was that you were issued a funnel and ledar hosen(short leather pants). The ledar hosen you wore to sneak back to West Germany and in case you did not make it back, the funnel made it easier to fill saltshakers in Siberia.

Don really enjoyed Berlin; it must have been his German heritage. While stationed at Templelhof Air Base in Berlin, he sang in the chapel choir and every other week they would make tape for a radio broadcast. These would be aired over the Armed Forces network into East Germany and East Berlin. During NATO meetings, the Russians would always complain about the radio programs.

Don was later stationed at a NATO base near Trier, Germany where Americans, Canadians, and French, operated the base. The Canadians always shared their good Canadian whisky and the French always carried a briefcase for their salami sandwiches and a bottle of wine for lunch.

The Crypto Center in the beginning was quite crude. It was two semi-trailers parked backend to backend with a pot-bellied stove in the middle. During the winter it was a bit cold . . . if any communications came in at night he had to start the fire to warm his fingers so he could type.

After ninety days Don was sent to the 50th Fighter/Bomber Wing, Hahn Air Force Base. This base was 40 miles from nowhere on a plateau above the Mossell River about 40 miles south of Koblence. He stayed here until he returned home and was discharged in January 1955.

Ronald Falkenham took basic Navy training at Great Lakes Training Center, Ill. in 1956 and became a communication technician with the rank of CT2 after which spent eighteen months in Turkey followed by a year in Germany.

He then received orders to a submarine in Italy and shipped out going north of the Soviet Union and staying for 40 days under the Arctic Ocean. "Best food I ever tasted!" he noted. This mission was classified. After his discharge in 1960 he went four years to Madison Business College.

During the Vienna Summit in June 1961, Khrushchev reiterated his threat to sign a separate peace treaty with East Germany if the West did not agree to his terms regarding Berlin by the end of the year. President Kennedy replied that it would be a "cold winter."

THE NEW "CHECK POINT CHARLIE"

On July 25 the President announced plans to meet the Soviet challenge in Berlin, including a powerful buildup of American conventional forces and finally drawing the line in the sand regarding Soviet Union interference with Allied access to West Berlin.

SAYING GOODBYE AT SOUTH BEAVER DAM

The Soviet Union and East Germany in turn deployed between 60 and 70 thousand troops around Berlin about August 12th 1961. The Berlin Wall Crisis so far had been limited to one event where a water canon used against NATO troops.

Thousands of troops are pulled from the U.S. to beef up forces in Europe. The tension was so serious the President

TROOP TRAIN MEDICAL SERVICES CAR

decided to call up additional reserves to replace them. On October 15, 1961, he ordered the Wisconsin National Guard (the Red Arrow Division) to active duty as part of the 148,000 member call-up of Reserve and Guard. This call up would impact Wisconsin hard with about 10,000 men being called up. Armories in 72 Wisconsin cities and towns scrambled to activate and get ready to go to Fort Lewis, Washington (near Tacoma) for training. Equipment would be loaded on 550 flatcars at 14 railroad sites in Wisconsin requiring up to 20 freight and troop trains. Fourteen light reconnaissance planes were to fly to Washington state, also.

WISCONSIN NATIONAL GUARD—32ND (RED ARROW) DIVISION COMPANY "E"

Members of the Beaver Dam Armory were ordered to report for duty on Oct. 15th 8:00 AM. **Capt. Dan (Don) Kordus** (company commander) announced a duty roster which put the Armory on a 24 hour alert basis. This first formation lasted about half an hour.

They were told they would be in Fort Lewis, Washington on or about the 27th, so they would

THE OLD BEAVER DAM ARMORY

leave from South Beaver Dam Oct 24 or 25, 1961. They were to report each day 7:30 AM for duty at the Armory until departure. Daily physical training would take place at Tahoe Park.

HAULING GEAR TO THE BAGGAGE CARS AT SOUTH BEAVER DAM

Work details were setup to pack all equipment, gear, and footlockers. Baggage railroad cars were sent by the military and placed on a siding in South Beaver Dam so gear was hauled from the Armory and packed in the baggage cars. Members were released to spend the weekend with their families. Public support and send-off programs by church and the city of Beaver Dam encouraged them until they left.

Company A of Waupun and Company E of Beaver Dam both left from South Beaver Dam on the same train. They eventually arrived in Fort Lewis, near Tacoma in the State of Washington and were housed in the old North Fort. The main

CONVOY TO SOUTH BEAVER DAM TROOP TRAIN

LOADING THE TRUCKS TO MOVE TO TRAIN...

fort was located a couple of miles south of their location where the 4th Division was stationed. The North Fort had not been occupied for several years and was in poor run-down condition. Poor living conditions and leaving home weighed heavily on the men so morale dipped to zero. However, they managed to improve on these conditions and with new busy training routines morale improved considerably over the next few months. There were only about 80 men in Company "E' when they left Beaver Dam, but it was soon brought up to full strength with the use of "fillers". Men were also ordered to active duty from various other military Reserve Centers in Minnesota, Wisconsin, and other mid-western states including several members of the Green Bay Packers and Minnesota Vikings. Ron Mayberry of the Vikings found himself in Company E.

Training was quite intense with a lot of field exercises. They trained away from camp for several days executing "Operation Bristlecone" in the Mojave Desert in California, maneuvering and playing war against the 1st Division from Fort Riley, Kansas. It was cold and windy causing severe sand storm like conditions therefore making it very difficult to carry out any kind of training exercises the first few days, but they stuck it out for a full seven days completing the exercise.

They also took part in "Operation Mesa Drive" about 108 miles east of Fort Lewis, Washington for a two week exercise against another unit from the National Guard.

Physical conditioning was a priority! Many of these field exercises were long and hazardous and of an obstacle course nature. Their physical condition was much improved by the time they returned home.

About 75% of the men were given ten (10) day furloughs to visit family in Beaver Dam for Christmas. Some were given five (5) day passes to be with family that had followed them to Fort Lewis and were living nearby for the duration.

As time went on, members of Congress and others began talking about an early release for the 32nd Division. The Berlin Crisis had cooled somewhat and it was felt the 32nd could stand-down. They were relieved of active duty in August 1962 after approximately 10 months of active duty.

THE "WALL"

On August 13 1961 the East German Government, supported by Khrushchev, closed the border between East and West Berlin by erecting the Berlin Wall and then went on to build fences and barriers to limit travel between Eastern Europe Soviet bloc communist countries and western democratic Europe. Although the citizens of Berlin reacted to the wall with outrage, many in the West (without doubt those within the Kennedy administration) were filled with relief. The wall interfered with the personal lives of the people but not with the political position of the Allies in Berlin. It was a "satisfactory" stalemate limiting both sides.

Bob Frankenstein was a young married man with a young 3 year old son and another baby daughter on the way.

The Cold War (counterfeit peace) after Korea had only bothered him occasionally, especially when he got alert notices in the mail to be ready to go on 24 hour notice or when the U.S. had another plane shot down in Korea. (He was in the reserves for six years after Korea)

He sometimes agonized if he should be building a special shelter for his family. Should he be storing more food and water? He really didn't have the money to do it and his military training and experience from Korea told him it was futile, but he had this gnawing feeling he should be doing something. He felt uncomfortable for not protecting his family in some way.

Emergency evacuation routes from Milwaukee and other large cities were being setup to get their people into country areas and government was putting food, medicine, and water into Beaver Dam buildings that might make a reasonable shelter.

Beaver Dam High School designed and gave out plans for home

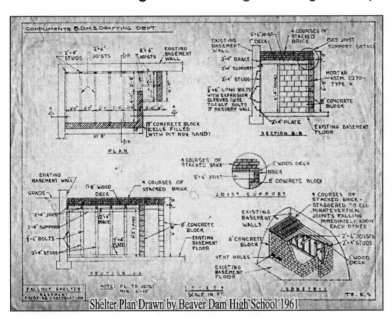

Shelter Plan Drawn by Beaver Dam High School 1961

basement shelters. The City of Beaver Dam had emergency plans setup and Beaver Dam schools held atom bomb drills in which our children would crawl under desks or go to basement rooms. ("Duck & Cover Drills") Everyone was told radiation would kill them unless they were below ground level or covered with thick earth. Radiation traveled in straight lines so below ground level was best.

Dave Kleindl of Beaver Dam was processed into the army through Fort Sheridan, Ill. He was assigned to Sugar Company of the 101st Airborne, Camp Breckenridge, Kentucky for 16 weeks of basic training. The Korean War truce was signed while he was in basic training.

After a short leave he reported to Camp Kilmer, New Jersey and shipped out of New York bound for Europe. They made several stops including Winston Salem, North Carolina, San Juan, Puerto Rico, and La Palme, France to pick up more troops before arriving at Bremerhaven, Germany 21 days later.

He was assigned to the 2nd Armored Cavalry Regiment with Headquarters in Nurnberg, Germany. He was stationed at Bindlach where he pulled border patrol duty along the East German and Czech borders from Hof to Arzberg rotating six weeks on the border and twelve weeks in training or maneuvers. The Regiment's mission was to train for war and conduct border surveillance.

THE FIRST OF MANY REFUGEES FLEEING EAST BERLIN WAS KILLED BY THE COMMUNISTS ON AUGUST 24, 1961

He tells of the eastern bloc soldiers inspecting the snow on their side in winter looking for tracks of possible escapees and in summer the land on their side was cultivated so they could find tracks in the loose dirt. They didn't trust their own guards so they had to check on them.

He also shares this tidbit with us. NATO heavy equipment and tanks were stored on an air strip at a nearby bombed-out WW II air field. The buildings above ground were destroyed, but underground there was a great network of domed rooms all connected that were untouched by bombing.

Background added by writer from Unit history The Regiment conducted gunnery training at Grafenwoehr, maneuver training at Hohenfels, later the Combat Maneuver Training Center, and participated in numerous (Return of Forces to Germany) exercises. The troops were constantly rehearsed to perform their portion of the NATO war plan. Throughout this era the Regiment was considered one of the most elite units of the entire Army and the best trained of the 300,000 soldiers stationed in Europe.

During the Cold War era the Second Armored Cavalry Regiment was responsible for surveillance of 731 kilometers along the Iron Curtain. Its sector included 375 kilometers of the border separating West and

THE DIVISION POINT BETWEEN THE EAST AND WEST WAS CALLED THE "IRON CURTAIN".

East Germany, as well as the entire 356 kilometers of the West German-Czechoslovakian border. From a distance, the border area appeared deceptively peaceful and scenic. Close inspection, however, revealed a massive and deadly barrier system. A series of metal mesh fences topped with barbed wire and equipped with sensitive warning devices, guard towers with interlocking fields of observation, and concrete walls similar to those found in Berlin presented a formidable barrier to freedom. Only a few legal-crossing points existed and these were heavily guarded and fortified. The East German and Czech border commands consisted of hand-picked individuals who were considered politically reliable and were well-trained in marksmanship and surveillance skills. The low number of successful escapes from East Germany, normally about 25 a year in the Second Armored Cavalry Regiment sector, testified to the deadly efficiency of the barrier system.

To conduct continuous border surveillance in sector, the Regiment operated six border camps in addition to the home garrisons of the squadrons. Camp Harris located in the town of Coberg, Kingsley Barracks in Hof, Camp Gates in Brand, Camp Pitman in Weiden, Camp Reed in Rutz, and Camp May in Regen. From the border camps, Second Second Armored Cavalry units patrolled their sectors by vehicle and on foot. Helicopters from the Fourth Squadron assisted from the air. At each border camp, a reaction force was kept on standby around the clock and could clear the camp within 15 minutes of the alert horn sounding. Finally the Regiment worked closely with the German border agencies, the Bundesgrenzshutz and Bavarian Border Patrol, and the Customs Police, sharing intelligence information and conducting joint patrols. The mission of the Regiment demanded the constant vigilance and dedication of all the soldiers stationed along the Iron Curtain.

Dave's comment on this experience; "Yes, we were separated from our families". He adds; "It was very hot and restricted during basic training and it was cold on night patrol or maneuvers during the winter in Germany, but it was like vacation when compared to men that were actually in combat or prisoners of war. Why some of us are granted such good fortune is a real mystery and is a lot to be thankful for."

Santa was short of sleighs on Christmas so they delivered presents to an orphanage with the half-track he was assigned to. The children sang some songs and they had treats. "That's the closest I came to be a hero" he said.

Cuban Crisis

According to Nikita Khrushchev's memoirs of May 1962 he considered placing

NIKITA KHRUSHCHEV

intermediate range missiles in Cuba as a means of countering the lead of the United States in developing and deploying missiles. He chose to use this deployment as a means of protecting Cuba from another United States sponsored

SOVIET MISSILE CONSTRUCTION IN CUBA

invasion, such as the failed attempt at the Bay of Pigs in 1961. The Soviet Union began building secret missile bases inside Cuba with Castro's approval.

On October 16, President Kennedy was briefed and shown U-2 spy plane

PRESIDENT KENNEDY

photographs of the missile installations in Cuba along with new intelligence that informed him that the Soviet Navy was on its way to supply Cuba with even more missiles. He ordered the military to full alert and U.S. missile systems moved to ready status. Military Command planes as was normal were already flying 24 hours a day with the idea if a ground command center was knocked out, the air commander in the plane could carry on. The clock to war was ticking!

On October 22, President Kennedy responded to this threat publicly by televising an address to the nation stating the discovery of the weapons and that any attack coming from Cuba would be treated as an attack directly by and from the Soviet Union. In addition he set a point of no return by imposing a naval blockade of Cuba to stop the construction of the sites.

Bob Frankenstein didn't know if he should go to work or stay home to protect his family. What if he got separated from his family? Would he ever find them again? Should he take his family out to his Dad's farm for safety? Bob was troubled! These worry thoughts were in the back of his mind much of the time.

President Kennedy announced that Cuba or the Soviets had shot down a U-2 spy plane over Cuba. War fever was rising and further enhanced by TV and radio practicing emergency announcements. Slowly time crawled by! When would the war start?

U-2 SPY PLANE

The President announced the Soviets were still sailing toward Cuba, steaming directly at the blockade lines set by our fleet. Our fleet had orders to stop them at all costs. Another day passed! The Soviets kept coming!

SOVIET SUBS WERE ALLOWED TO SURFACE
AFTER THE CRISIS.

The Soviets had previously hidden diesel powered submarines with nuclear tipped missiles in the Gulf of Mexico. Our navy fleet found and literally sat on top of each them thus trapping them far below forcing their inhabitants to breath increasingly more toxic air and depriving them of radio communication with the Soviet Union. Would they panic and attempt to fire nuclear missiles?

On October 26, Khrushchev sent a letter to Kennedy suggesting that the sites would be dismantled if the United States gave its reassurance that it would not invade Cuba. The United States agreed and in turn the U.S. would quietly drop planned missiles sites on the Soviet Union border in or near Turkey.

Following this; on October 28, Khrushchev announced that the Cuban sites would be dismantled along with the removal of light bombers and the Soviet fleet would be recalled.

It (the total destruction of the earth) had been so close that the two countries now decided to install special direct crisis phones to prevent an accidental nuclear war.

The Cold War (this counterfeit peace) continued to smolder in other parts of the world including Vietnam and South America. Both sides were back to surrogate wars again and these areas would suck in our advisers and troops putting them in harm's way. This one is called Vietnam!

VIETNAM

SOME AREA SOLDIERS KILLED IN ACTION

David B. Merrill KIA January 9th, 1967   Kenneth L. Schaefer KIA July 3, 1966
Roger C. Ackerman KIA May 7th 1968   Robert A. Kreuziger KIA April 6th, 1966
Ralph A. Dahm Feb. 8th, 1968   Stephen J. Westphal April 13th 1968

This undeclared war was inherited from the French. It was a French colony up to and during WW II until they lost it to Japan. After the defeat of Japan the French again moved in to reclaim French Indochina. The French had invested in rubber plantations, minerals, etc. and did not want to give up these rich resources. After WW II these French Indochinese countries wanted independence from the French so the communists took up this cause to empower themselves and their political goals. The French finally gave up fighting after many set-backs and the U.S. decided fill this vacuum of power before the communists could take over that part of the world.

The French Indochina War ended with a symbolic 1954 Geneva brokered 17th Parallel DMZ between North and South Vietnam. They were to hold eventual joint free elections and unify under a duly elected government.

However the north like in Korea decided they would do this only under communism without a free election and so a civil war started.

The U.S. started helping the south with small groups of military advisers about February 1961. It would eventually grow into a huge military operation of many years. **Howard Abel** of Beaver Dam was a member of the Green Berets and a part of the Special Forces with Ranger Training. He was there as an advisor to the South Vietnamese military. One day he was accidently shot in the leg while engaged in horseplay with friends in Vietnam. His work was secret so not much is known.

The U.S. and South Vietnam won the military battles but never won the hearts and minds of the people. This country had been under the control of others for decades and the nationalistic people who simply wanted to rule themselves were convinced Communism might be the highway to achieve it.

"Search and Discover Patrols" were somewhat different in Korea. Korea was a peninsula surrounded and isolated by sea water on three sides while Vietnam was bordered by several countries where secret armies and supplies could be hidden. In Korea helicopters were new and very basic used mostly for medical rescue and limited troop moving but in Vietnam they were developed into sophisticated medical evacuation systems, gunships with powerful rocket launchers, major troop carriers, and helicopter cranes used to carry heavy equipment. Like Korea U.S. planes also ruled the air and U.S. ships garrisoned the sea and protected South Vietnam ports but the many rivers and trails also had to be patrolled that connected with bordering countries.

In Korea troops were trucked, marched, or parachuted into position whereas in Vietnam one to hundreds of helicopter gunships loaded with troops and supplies would drop them into position from home base and return to home base.

U.S. strategy included setting up central fortified posts, garrisoned nearby villages and military outposts with the resulting circles of

PATROL CRASH SCENE

influence around each area. It was hoped the surrounding villages would respond to this umbrella of relative safety and medical care with loyalty to democratic south rather than communist north. "Search and Destroy Patrols" from these bases and outposts visited local villages and searched the countryside for communists forces and supply activity. Information derived from local patrol operations was then sent to the rear for intelligence to analyze and used to set-up squad to multi-battalion sized Search and Destroy operations in the future. Unlike Korea where frontlines and outposts were directly attacked by the enemy, these mobile operations were routine in Vietnam where the hidden and invisible enemy had to be hunted out.

SEARCHING A TUNNEL

The communist strategy made the south come to it on its own terms and included communist infiltrators living and mingling with the villagers holding families members hostage if they didn't cooperate, killing village elders, and blending nationalism with communism to win the minds and cooperation of the Vietnamese people and playing on the fact that more than anything else nationalist Vietnamese wanted their own country and peace!

Their strategy also included a hidden army that lived in forests, tunnels, and caves. This army would appear and disappear and choose its battles. Highly populated undeveloped countries have the greatest of resources; unlimited people! They could practice attrition, that is loose twenty soldiers to one of ours and they would eventually wear us down and win. Individual members of this hidden army did not expect to live to ever return home and could live off the land.

This was the challenge for the Americans. America needed to convince millions of nationalistic people who wanted their very own country that they would be better off a democratic based country than a communists based country.

There were many pitfalls to overcome to achieve this. Living generation after generation under the control of foreign countries the Vietnamese people did not fathom democracy or communism and had no real idea how to govern themselves. They were a part of old world culture with simple needs and simple ways and feared these changes pushed by people who did not speak their language, who did not look like them, and who it appeared not respect their culture. Like Korea and almost every other colony seeking self-rule after WW II this would mean a tragic civil war caught between two political philosophies or sometimes competing religions trying to limit the spread and influence of the other.

Timothy A. Kasmiskie was a 1966 graduate of the Beaver Dam High School. He then joined and served in the U.S. Army in Vietnam. He was in Able and Charley Companies and a part of the 1st Cavalry operations in Nam.

He received four Purple Hearts, three Bronze Stars, Air Medal, Silver Star and other decorations. He was a member of the Watertown Post of the VFW, Disabled American Veterans, Order of the Purple Heart, and the 1st Cavalry Association. He had served his country!

Vietnam was war conducted by an elusive enemy seen only when they wanted to be seen. They were known as the North Vietnam Army (NVA) plus there were thousands of communist sympathizers Viet Cong (VC) slipping in and living in secret in the south. They blended in with civilians and hid their weapons bringing them out only when they wanted. They were supported by two major communist nations (China and Soviet Union) seeking to bring them into the communist spear of influence.

Communist forces always had their back to the sun and used many old world inexpensive methods to fight modern weapons. They successfully used the jungle, rice paddies, poison punji sticks, and booby traps with deadly skill.

They used munitions bearers, underground tunnel travel, underground hospitals, underground warehousing, and a underground military supply support system along with underground command centers with great skill.

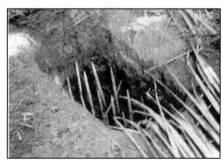

PUNJI STICK TRAP

Propaganda tied to a dream for independence drove them all on. They conducted a terror and intimidation war on civilians to keep them in line while living and hiding among them.

They were also masters at setting up firefights from inside or near villages or civilian areas and when the U.S. or Arvin protected themselves, they would slip away making it look to the world like the Americans were deliberately killing harmless families and children. This type of propaganda successfully demonized the democratic south while showing communist North Vietnamese as a saviors.

TRANSPORT OPERATIONS COULD INCLUDE UP TO 500 HELICOPTERS

For every action taken in war there is a counter action. To limit supplies from North Vietnam the U.S. had to cut those routes to the south. River routes had to be controlled with special gun boat patrols, but this was then countered by supply routes through the jungle. Jungle routes had to be patrolled and cut. These routes were exposed using agent orange (a defoliant) and were patrolled and bombed mercilessly to cut the supply. Then miles of supply and support tunnel routes were dug by NKA and VC and in turn dogs and American soldiers called tunnel rats were trained to find, clear, and destroy them.

TUNNEL RATS AND THEIR DOGS

Daily patrols would be sent out on search and destroy missions to seek out these supply line routes or to contain or control the NVA. These patrols were met with deadly booby-trapped trails, ambushes, punji sticks and the enemy slipping away to hide. U.S. outposts were hit with deadly heavy armament hand carried from the north. Road blocks setup for vehicle inspections further alienated the general population.

PATROL LOOKING FOR VIETCONG

There were so many civilian casualties that none of this effort would help to create the mindset needed to form a free nation.

This same technique used by the communists in Vietnam to vilify the Americans was used in the states. Laws already protect conscientious objectors and certain religions allowing them do alternate non-military service and during this time period

college students were exempted from the draft so many of those seeking to avoid the military became sham students while others skipped out to Canada. Still others became mail order clergy to avoid the draft. Thus only the most dedicated and loyal young people chose to serve their country in Vietnam.

More and more children and young adults were moved by the press and peers to distrust the

PROTESTING THE WAR—RIOT CONTROL

establishment. A research building in Madison, Wisconsin was bombed, massive public demonstrations, and civil disobedience became poplar activities nationwide. Youth would deliberately bait and draw police or the military into a confrontation always to make the establishment look like the bad guy.

In Vietnam, frustration created unwise decisions and a so called daily body count. The press became so opinionated they focused on a baby killed and not on the number of village families protected. Reading about themselves in the press releases (about the war effort in Vietnam) became

STERLING HALL BLAST

unbearable to many GIs who turned to drink or used drugs to cope. They were called baby-killers and worse! They had the negative spotlight rather than honoring gallant soldiers who saved lives, delivered babies, and protected children, while on patrol. Goals were unclear with an ending unknown so there was only one goal; survive today, celebrate each day, and live to go home. *Do what it takes to go home!*

The war lasted so long that certain bases in Vietnam evolved into recreation centers complete with sand beaches and night clubs from which people left for work (patrols) each morning and returned each night. It was an eerie baffling war with one way of living and coping inside base and another desperate life in the countryside.

Charles Staab enlisted and would spent his 19th birthday and first day in the service at the Great Lakes Naval Training Center, Great Lakes, Illinois. He could have left later for basic (July) but thought with the heat and humidity of summer it might be better to go earlier and thus give himself a break. While in basic he served as a Seaman Recruit.

On July 12, 1966 he graduated from basic as a Seaman Apprentice and was given orders to the Naval Justice School, Newport, R.I. He was going to go to Commissary School (cook)(also in Newport) and was wearing what they called a striker badge. It was a spoon crossed with a pen quill and was the badge for commissary. Not knowing how to read orders at this point, he asked a someone on the base bus where he should get off. Upon reading the orders, he told Charles to get off on the next corner, adding that Charles

PUNJI STICKS

should take off the striker badge as he wasn't going to Commissary School.

Charles was assigned to the Naval Justice School. He had no idea what that was but found out early in the Navy that you can't always believe what you are told. Guess they needed Legal Yeoman more than cooks.

After seven weeks of school, he stayed on as staff at the school tutoring and acting as an instructors aide. He had graduated 15th out of 67. Legal Yeoman (Office Clerk) take care of recording documents and writs pertaining to court martial, larger captain masts, similar to a court recorder (stenographer) on the outside. Procedures are different in the gathering of needed information with a different system (closed microphone). It requires coordinating, listening, typing, and recording it all down on a disc that looked like a floppy 45 rpm record. He took typing in school and at that time pounded out about 65 wpm. His record showed this so he surmised this is what got him in this predicament. He didn't like the fact he wasn't going to be a cook, but he found this to be an interesting job and they told him rank could come much faster in this specialized field and on August 14, 1966 he was promoted to Seaman.On May

26, 1967 he was given orders to his next duty assignment, the USS Arnold J. Isbell (DD869), 132 Division, Seventh fleet ported out of Long Beach, CA. After a 30 day leave, he reported aboard the Isbell on August 15, 1967 and assumed his duties as Legal Yeoman in the Ship's Office. He also assumed the duties of Classified Material Yeoman, Mail Yeoman and the (CO) Commanding Officer's personal Yeoman. He took care of Officer Records and all personal correspondence to and from the

USS ARNOLD J. ISBELL

Commanding Officer and Exec. As a new Yeoman aboard, with less time than the other Yeoman and personnel men he felt over whelmed by all the duties he was given.

He thinks some of the guys with more time thought he knew someone or something to have gotten so much recognition. He did what was expected of him and to the best of his knowledge it was appreciated by his peers.

After about a year of updates in dry dock, refresher training, and shakedown cruises, they were issued orders to Vietnam on what was referred to as a WESTPAC Cruise. They set sail for Hawaii on July 15, 1968, with a stop in Guam for further supplies.

On July 17, 1968 he was promoted to YN3 (E-4). From Guam they continued on to Yokosuka, Japan, Hong Kong, Kaohsiung, Taiwan, and finally to Vietnam.

They patrolled north of the Cua Viet River near the DMZ for firing missions in support of the Third Marine Division. The Isbell participated in Operation Sea Dragon firing over 2,215 rounds on enemy targets destroying 8 bunkers, 8 artillery and mortar positions, structures, buildings, with 3 wounded and 36 killed in action during the first two days on the firing line. She was equipped with two 5"/38 caliber gun mounts.

They went on to rescue a downed spotter plane pilot near the Ben Hai River in South China Sea and she was one of the last two destroyers in the area to take out coastal gun emplacements ending Operation Sea Dragon. By the time they finished their tour off the shores of Vietnam, they had delivered over 8,000 rounds to enemy targets. They returned to south of the DMZ for further orders.

While waiting for orders they had the privilege of meeting Major John Isbell, who was stationed in South Vietnam and was flown by copter to the ship which had been named after his father. They were told Captain Isbell was killed on board the USS Franklin during the Korean War. It was a pleasure to meet him and to this day he never heard about him again.

During his stay off the coast of Vietnam, Chuck was ordered to Naval Support out of Chu Lai—Da Nang for court martial proceedings. (temporary additional duty) He also served aboard the River Patrol Boat (PBR532) on temporary additional duty. (TAD)

He also volunteered for up-river surveillance duty which had nothing to do with his job description. Crew members really needed a rest and asked for volunteers. The Isbell went on to serve in many other capacities during their WESTPAC Cruise. After over seven months at sea, they returned home via Singapore, Subic Bay, Philippines, Hong Kong, Yokosuka, stopping at Australia for R&R finally arriving back at Long Beach on January 31, 1969.

RIVER BOAT PATROLLING INLAND WATERS

Early separation requests were being distributed so he decided to take advantage of it. On January 9, 1970 he was released to Naval Reserves inactive duty and honorably discharged on March 6, 1972.

During his tour with the Navy, he was awarded to Navy/USMC Achievement, US Vietnam Service, Vietnam Campaign, Combat Action, Good Conduct, Navy Expert Pistol, and the National Defense Service Ribbon/Medal plus citations and commendations from local commands and Seventh Fleet.

Alvin Steffen of Beaver Dam was nearing the end of his military career. He was now stationed in Chicago on special detail with several others and lived in a hotel. They had the devastating duty to notify families of the loss of a loved one and to support the family by arranging for the military part of the funeral.

Dan Klossner of Juneau was drafted into the Army in 1969. He would be trained an extra 10 weeks as a Medic. He was then sent to Vietnam on a chartered Flying Tiger Airline. Upon arriving he remembers a simple sign in the airport that read; "You never live until you almost die."

He was issued his jungle fatigues, helmet, and M-16, and assigned to a company in which he would accompany infantry search and destroy ground patrols. Things were fairly normal for about two months during which they would sometimes hold sick call in the villages. He did deliver a baby, cure infections, and comfort children injured by weapons of war.

Then one day in early April (about two months after his arrival) they were sent on a body retrieval recon patrol and airlifted by helicopter to a location in the jungle. Supplied with the needed body bags they dropped about six foot to the ground from the chopper. Choppers usually did not land on grounds that might be mined and staying in hover position allowed for instant getaway.

They spread out forming two lines (each with a point man) and proceeded into the jungle to find the bodies. They didn't realize the bodies were being used as bait for an ambush. The point men were almost at the other side of a little clearing when they were fired on. Both point men were hit (one was his best friend) so he as medic was needed on both lines. He could see his friend who appeared to be holding his hand up so he crawled over to help him. Dan was almost there when he was hit in the forehead with a bullet that went out the side of his head. He continued over to his friend, found him severely hit and suffering two broken legs, and attempted to drag him toward

MEDIC AT WORK

the rear. His friend informed him it was no use and asked Dan to pray with him and then died. While doing this Dan was shot again; the bullet entering his right buttocks shattering bone in both legs. The enemy then used him as bait to draw others to help him so they could be killed. They were in desperate condition when finally rescued by gunships.

Blood from the wounded was dripping out the doors of the gunships as they were taken to a field hospital and then on to Japan. His legs were both encased and locked to each other for six and a half months. While in Japan he was overwhelmed with malaria. He would have three operations on his head and now has a plastic plate in his head. He was able to spend most of his hospital time recovering at the nearby Great Lakes Naval Hospital.

He received a nice welcome locally, but while going to school at the University of Wisconsin he was the object of disrespect. He was spat in the face once and replied by knocking the man down. The police were called and asked who started the fight? The man said that Dan had served in Vietnam so he spit on him. The cop said it was a fair fight and left.

Roger Klug of Beaver Dam enlisted in May of 1968. He took Marine Corp training at San Diego, Calif. and finished boot camp as a Pfc in August of 1968. He then was sent to Camp Pendleton for more grunt training after which was shipped to Vietnam and arrived January 19th, 1969. He arrived just in time for the Tet Offensive. He and his buddies were under sniper and rocket attack and had to fight for their very lives.

TET OFFENSIVE

By the grace of God, he returned safely to the USA in June of 1970. He eventually received an honorable discharge. He finds it very difficult to talk about his experience.

Author's partial letter to Roger . . . I am going to share a few thoughts with you as I understand you are still struggling with the mind games of combat. These wounds of the mind are deep and mean! In front of me is your very special story. It is the story of a gentleman who served his country in Vietnam. This gentleman is from Beaver Dam. This gentleman is you! There was no way you could know it at the time, but the cost to carry on the Vietnam War would help break up the Communist block of countries. It was one of the main reasons the old Soviet Union disintegrated. Afghanistan finished that break-up! Veterans from

FIRE AND DEATH OF THE TET OFFENSIVE

Nam achieved incredible goals, but suffered severe political losses completely out of their control.

Veterans of Nam were some of the best soldiers ever put in the field!

Many veterans like you hold pent-up memories of themselves in desperate situations and feel unwarranted guilt for surviving. They were alarmed to discover that

GUNSHIP RESCUE

the basic survival instinct in all of us moved them to do actions that seemed to defy; the teachings of their youth, family, and church.

Combat is terror, turmoil, and violence! It is cold, desperate, and personal! Losing a buddy and then another and another . . . makes it difficult to ever allow yourself a close friend again. Many vets were afraid to be close, even to family for years, for fear they might suffer the hurt and guilt of losing them. Marriage would not be possible for many.

Can you imagine a veteran returning home from The Civil War? It was friend against friend and family against family, state against state!

Life of a returning veteran is a mixture of personal pride, guilt, heroism, national pride, loyalty, and sometimes disdain. Life is not perfect! Veterans coming home sought to share these incredible feelings with other veterans by joining the American Legion, Veterans of Foreign Wars, and other service clubs. These clubs did nice things for children, families, and other veterans . . . helping each other adjust back to civilian life. War veterans were the only ones who can understand these feelings. Best wishes in the future. Post Script, I am including your important story in my book.

Dear Bob,
I proof read and want to thank you for your insight Thank you + GoD Bless You
Roger Kln

Tet Offensive The Tet holiday had traditionally been a time of truce in the long war and both communist Hanoi and democratic Saigon had made announcements that this year would be no different.

The following (taken from public records) is used to tell the typical story of Vietnam. January 31st, the first day of the Vietnamese New Year, the National Liberation Front (NLF) also known as communist guerilla forces (Viet Cong) and North Vietnamese Army (NVA) attacked most every important village and larger city in South Vietnam including important American bases. They had been hidden in tunnels, safe houses and jungle.

These attacks came as a total surprise to most both soldiers and civilians. Inhabitants

SELF-DESTRUCTION OF WAR

of cities and villages were now being "liberated" by thousands of gun-waving NVA/VC marching through the streets proclaiming success of their great communist revolution, while their death squads quickly rounded up hit lists of collaborators and South Vietnam government sympathizers for street trials and instant executions.

Mean-while some nineteen Viet Cong blew their way through the outer walls of the US Embassy and ran head-on into the five MP's (Military Police) on duty early that morning. Two MP's were killed as the VC attempted to blow their way through the heavy inner embassy doors using anti-tank rockets. Not only was that a failure, but they found themselves pinned-down by concentrated fire from the courageous marine guards. An additional force of US 101st Airborne was radioed in and landed by helicopter. Nineteen VC were soon dead, strewn around the embassy grounds plus five Americans and two Vietnamese civilians. The communist commandos dressed in civilian clothing had driven to the embassy in an old vehicle. Security of the embassy was not in doubt after the first few minutes and the damage was insignificant.

This attack on "American soil" captured the imagination of the media and the battle became symbolic of the Tet Offensive throughout the world.

Sections of each stricken city were soon reduced to rubble in heavy street by street fighting. Tanks, helicopter gunships, and strike aircraft would hit parts of each city or village containing entrenched guerrillas until they would slip away into the surrounding villages and fight from there. US and ARVN troops had to drive them out of these theoretically pacified villages to reoccupy them. The NVA/VC repeated this ploy many times forcing the Saigon Government destroy their own villages and by

THE SHAMBLES OF WAR

doing so, furthering alienation of the population. Estimates put the number of civilian dead at some 15,000 and the number of new refugees at anything up to two million and it still raged on.

The success of the Tet holiday offensive was erratic. Many of the attacks on the provincial cities and U.S. bases were easily beaten back while others were tortuous vicious fighting.

While in temporary control of an area the National Liberation Front and Viet-Cong carried on a "liberation" program. Thousands of South Vietnam communist prisoners were set free and thousands of "enemies of North Vietnam" such as government officials, sympathizers, and Catholics were arrested and many were shot on orders from National Liberation Front which had sent in its death squads with prepared hit-lists. Most of the others simply vanished.

At the end of February South Vietnamese officials sifting through the rubble found mass graves with over 1200 corpses and sometime later other mass burials in the provincial areas. The total number of bodies unearthed came to around 2500 but the number of civilians estimated as missing after the battle was nearly 6000. Many of the victims found were Catholics who sought sanctuary in church but were taken out and shot. Others were apparently being marched off for political "re-education" but were shot when American or ARVN units came too close.

The mass graves within Hue itself were largely of those who had been picked up and executed for various "enemy of the people" offenses. There is some doubt that the National Liberation Front and Viet-Cong had planned all these executions beforehand but without question it was the largest communist purge of the war.

Dennis Brest was in the service in 1970 serving as a supply specialist. It was his responsibility to keep weapons clean and inventoried while working as a quartermaster supply clerk.

Michael Smith of Beaver Dam was part of an Armor company in Germany about 1972. He was part of M60A1 tank crew for 3 years. He could perform in all positions except tank commander. Many years later he would also serve in Iraq. He is a part of the Army reserves in Beaver Dam.

This is a story about **a Viet Nam vet and Ann Margaret** as told by the vet's wife. (Source unknown) Richard, (her husband), never really talked a lot about his time in Viet Nam in 1966 other than he had been shot by a sniper. However, he had a rather grainy, 8 x 10 black and white photo he had taken at a USO show featuring Ann Margaret with Bob Hope in the background, that was one of his treasures.

A few years ago, Ann Margaret was doing a book signing at a local bookstore. Richard wanted to see if he could get her to sign the treasured photo so he arrived at the bookstore at 12 o'clock noon for the 7:30 PM signing.

By the time she got there the line went all the way around the bookstore circled the parking lot and disappeared behind a parking garage. Before her appearance, bookstore employees announced that she would sign only her book and no memorabilia would be permitted.

Richard was disappointed, but wanted to show her the photo and let her know how much those shows meant to lonely GI's so far from home. Ann Margaret came out looking as beautiful as ever and as second in line it was soon Richard's turn.

He presented the book for her signature and then took out the photo. When he did there were many shouts from the store employees that she would not sign it. Richard said, "I understand. I just wanted her to see it."

She took one look at the photo, tears welled up in her eyes and she said, "This is one of my gentlemen from Viet Nam and I most certainly will sign his photo. I know what these men did for their country and I always have time for "my gentlemen."

ANN MARGRET IN VIETNAM

With that, she pulled Richard across the table and planted a big kiss on him. She then made quite a to-do about the bravery of the young men she had met over the years, how much she admired them, and how much she appreciated them. There weren't too many dry eyes among those close enough to hear. She then posed for pictures and acted as if he was the only one there.

Later at dinner, Richard was very quiet. When I asked if he'd like to talk about it, her big strong husband broke down in tears. "That's the first time anyone ever thanked me for my time in the Army," he said.

That night was a turning point for him. He walked a little straighter and, for the first time in years, was proud to have been a Vet. She said she will never forget Ann Margaret for her graciousness and how much that small act of kindness meant to her husband.

THE USS GARRETT COUNTY

Harvey Lewis would link up with his ship in Guam in late January 1969 and then sail to Subic Bay in the Philippines. On the way, there they had 40 MM gun practice on 55 gallon drums, that were set adrift in the ocean. They tried, but the drums bobbed around too much to ever hit one. They finally had to sink them with 50 caliber machine gun fire.

They stayed in Subic Bay a couple of weeks or so and after picking up supplies and parts for the PBR's (Patrol Boat River), they headed off to Vietnam. On the way to Vietnam, they again took 40 MM gun practice on calmer seas. They did finally hit and sink a couple of the 55 gallon drums after many tries. This made the old man (the captain) happy.

They arrived in Vietnam in late February, 1969 and went up the Mekong river to a small city called Ven Long.

The USS Garrett County (LST 786) would serve as a "mother ship" for river patrol people,

BROWN WATER PATROL BOATS

called the US Riverine Forces. The versatile LST was well-suited to this role, with generous space for stores, repair shops, and berthing.

In addition to the numerous small craft seen alongside, she also supported the helicopters that operated with the Riverine Forces. The clear, flat main deck of the LST served as a useful landing platform for medium helicopters. This ship would eventually be reclassified as a patrol craft tender (AGP), a designation previously carried by several ex-seaplane tenders.

HELICOPTER ON DECK

The smaller brown water patrol boats were equipped with a variety of armament designed to cope with the enemy on the river. These small craft were used to neutralize any attempt by the Viet Cong to control the river for bringing in supplies.

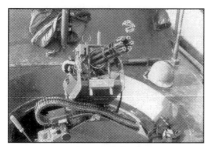

GATLING GUN

While cruising up and down the river, crews stopped and inspected native river transportation vehicles for arms or equipment that might aid the enemy. They also supported our troops on land during enemy (VC) action along the river and in turn took hits from sappers, shore guns, and snipers.

THE "MOTHER SHIP"

After each mission they returned to their tender, in this case, the USS Garrett County (LST 786) for repair, supplies, refueling, and food and rest for the crews.

This in turn made the tenders a prime target. Navy Seal action and helicopter gunships were frequently used in a defense mode.

The USS Garrett County was equipped with formidable fire power and was used to support many river assault operations against VC and North Vietnamese troops.

Stateside people seeing the reality of war for the first time on nightly television soon sickened of war and wanted out. The media both correctly informed or betrayed the American people as blinded by their own bias. Politicians running for office created further deliberately created doubt and division for their own advantage. Eventually the establishment's police and soldiers would become the enemy and communist sympathizers in this country took advantage of this division to push their agenda. Soon America was blundering about without

LOSS OF HOME FRONT SUPPORT

credible leadership and tangible goals thus losing the support of its youth, losing the will to succeed and leaving some of the bravest and best-trained soldiers we have ever had in Vietnam without national direction or home front support. These brave men and women who had fought and died so valiantly for this country now had to adjust their mind-set from hero to leper. Disrespect devastated them to their very souls, crippling many for the rest of their lives.

America eventually starting phasing out military involvement gradually turning the war over to the South Vietnamese. The Paris Peace Accords ending the conflict was signed January 27, 1973.

About 2 years after this the South would falter thus allowing the Communist north to move in. The South surrendered April 30, 1975. Thirty years of war was finally over.

The U.S. suffered 58,119 killed, 153.303 wounded and 1948 missing in action. The South Vietnamese loss 230,000 killed with 1,169,763 wounded. The North lost about 1,100,000 and unknown wounded.

A FADING DREAM

The people of that part of the world, were about to lose almost as many lives than all the previous 30 years of war. Purge after purge of Vietnam and adjoining countries resulted in millions of deaths, loss of whole ethnic cultures, and mountains of human bones. Dreams of free independence became Communist enslavement of both mind and body.

COMMUNISM AND ITS REWARDS

In Cambodia alone 21% of the country's population would be wiped out during the purge or 1.7 million. In Laos the Pathet Lao joined up with the communists of North Vietnam and after North Vietnam's takeover of South Vietnam and Cambodia in 1975, the Pathet Lao (now officially the Lao People's Revolutionary Party) gained military and thus political control over the entire country. Over 30% of the Hmong people were killed after 1975 and about 30% fled to and settled in the US including Wisconsin.

PLEASE HELP ME! WHICH ONES ARE MY MOM OR DAD?

Only now, many years after the cold war, do we find documents from the old Soviet Union and the countries they controlled in Europe, how much this war contributed to their collapse! We are just now realizing the full value of the brave "Nam" veteran. We pulled them out from that dreadful conflict, but we won the cold war! Thank God they did their part!

1989 Counterfeit Peace (Cold War) implosion

LEFT -PRESIDENT RONALD REAGAN
SEC. GENERAL MIKHAIL GORBACHEV
"MELTING THE COLD WAR"

The United States of Soviet Republics (USSR) political myth fell apart disintegrating into separate states. Communism had failed to compete with the freedom and energy of the West. It was now a desperately poor humiliated Russia. The new Russia was a much better member of the world family of nations. The facade was gone.

1989, The Berlin Wall came down resulting in the unification of East and West Germany in 1990.

The naïve, abandoned mostly leaderless countries of the old Soviet Union faced new evils while recreating a new states for themselves: political corruption, inflation, inefficiency, poor infrastructure, unemployment, unskilled labor, food shortages, and old suppressed ethnic conflicts, would haunt them. It was the pandemonium that surrounded the collapse of the Soviet Union . . . allowed to run its course by a thoughtful Gorbachev doing what he thought was best . . . that compounded the many problems of the restored independent countries of Eastern Europe.

The charade of communism was visible for all to see so these restored nations would look to the west for inspiration.

This author worked long and hard to seek out local veteran's stories and to use them to tell the history of our nation. Certain parts of the cold war period are missing because local veterans chose not to or could not talk about their military life during those times.

ALWAYS REMEMBER THE "MISSING IN ACTION" AND "PRISONER OF WAR" SOLDIER.

VETERAN'S HONOR ROLL OF SERVICE FOR THIS COMMUNITY PARTIAL LIST FOR SEVERAL WARS AND CONFLICTS

HOWARD E.	ABEL	ARMY USA IC	1961-64
ROGER	ACKERMAN	ARMY S/SGT	KIA VIETNAM
H. F.	ALBRECHT	NAVY BATTLESHIP	WW II
H. J.	ALBRECHT	AIR FORCE C. E.	VIETNAM
ALAN	ALBRECHT	AIR FORCE	VIETNAM
MARVIN	ALDERDEN	ARMY CPL MECH.	KOREA-1952-53
LYNN B	ANDERSON	MARINE CORP	VIETNAM
JOHN H.	ANDERSON	ARMY ENGINEER	VIETNAM 1968-69
THOMAS	ANDERSON	ARMY MEDIC	GERMANY 1952-54
PAUL S.	ANDORFER	MARINE	VIETNAM
ANDREW	ANFINSON	NAVY S/1	WW II
HARVEY A.	ANSAY	AIR FORCE CM/SGT	1941-1968
WM. E.	ARNDORFER	INF. SUP. CO. 53	WAGONER-WW I
WM. J.	ARNDORFER	ARMY 9TH ARMOR	BRONZE STAR-WW II
ROBERT	ARNDORFER	ARMY PFC	10TH ARMOR-WW II
DONALD	ARNDORFER	ARMY PFC 4TH DIV.	EUROPE-1951-53
RALPH	ARNDORFER	ARMY SFC 25TH DIV.	KOREA-1952-54
PAUL	ARNDORFER	ARMY CO. CLERK	EUROPE-1953-55
RUSS	ARVOLD	MARINE MAJOR	WW II
DONALD	ASCHAKER	NAVY MECHANIC	WW II 1944-47
MONNIE A.	AUBRY	ARMY SP/4	VIETNAM 1971-72
JOHN R.	AUKOFER	NAVY RADARMAN	WW II
PAUL H.	BAARS	AF MISSILE SYS.	COLD WAR
JOHN W.	BACH	MARINE SGT	KOREA
EUGENE	BAGNESKI	ARMY PVT. 89TH MTN.	K.I.A. WW II
PAUL L.	BAKER	AIR FORCE T/SGT	WW II 1940-45
ROBERT G.	BAKER	MARINE	WW II 1943-46
S. R.	BALLIETTE	NAVY AIR CORP	WW II
TED	BARTELL	ARMY SGT.	WW I 1915-20
RUSSELL	BARTON	ARMY ENGINEER	WW II 1942-45
GERALD	BASKFIELD	ARMY	1953-56
MARK J.	BASKFIELD	ARMY	1981-83
JOHN J.	BASZYNSKI	ARMY FA T/SGT	WW II 1943-45
BERT	BASZYNSKI	ARMY TANK SGT.	WW II
CRAIG	BASZYNSKI	A.F. MISSILE TECH.	GERMANY 1963-67
JAMES W.	BATH	US NAVY EM3MS	PACIFIC WW II 1942-45
MICHAEL H.	BATH	MARINE	KOREA
JOHN T. W.	BAUMANN	MERCHANT MARINE	AMMO SHIPS-WW II
BRIAN V.	BEAMER	NAVY SEABEES CM	1982-2002
JAN M.	BEAMER	NAVY SEABEES SWC	1985-2006
EDWARD J.	BEARDER	ARMY	1943
MICHAEL	BECKER	ARMY SGT. 214 FA	GERMANY 1969-71
JOHN M.	BECKER	PHARMACIST/MATE	NAVY WW II
ELMER C.	BECKER	NAVY SK 2/C	WW II-1942-45
MILES P.	BEDKER	NAVY S 1/C GUNNER	WW II 1943-46
ROBERT N.	BEDKER	ARMY INFANTRY	WIA-BRZSTAR-WW II
KENNETH	BEDKER	ARMY	WW II 1946-47
JOHN A.	BEDKER	SCARWAF ENG.	COLD WAR 1954-56

WILLIAM	BEECHER	COAST GUARD	WW II
AP	BEECHER JR	ARMY TECH	WW II 1941-45
JEAN A.	BEERS	USN WAVE Y 2/C	WW II
ERNST	BEHNISCH	ARMY RANGER CPL.	PACIFIC WW II
ERVIN R.	BEILFUSS	SIGNAL CORP	KOREA-1949-52
DONALD A.	BEILFUSS	USAF A & E MECH.	KOREA-1952-53
JOEY L.	BEMIS	AIR FORCE SGT	1977-81
CARMEN	BEMIS	NAVY WAVES	1945-46
LLOYD G.	BEMIS	NAVY MN/1	1941-1968
FRED L.	BENEDITZ	ARMY PFC	WW I
GORDON	BENIKE	USAF MECHANIC	1955-59
GENE F.	BENIKE	NAVY SONARMAN 3	WW II USS GEARING
GLENN G.	BENNETT	MARINE CORPORAL	1954-57
ART. J.	BENNETT JR.	ARMY QM/USAR	SFC. 1950-56
LEROY	BENNINGER	ARMY SIG. CORP T/4	WW II 1942-45
BENNY W.	BENSLEY	ARMY S/SGT	POW WW II
LLOYD	BERENT	NAVY AF M/SGT.	WW II & KOREA
MERRILL J.	BERG	ARMY 32ND DIV.	SO. PACIFIC WW II
DAVID	BERG	ARMY 1969-72	VIETNAM ERA
DAN	BERKEVICH	MARINE SGT.	GULF WAR 1985-91
RUSSELL A.	BERNDT	AIR FORCE COOK	1962-66
GUST. W.	BERNDT	ARMY AIR CORP SGT.	WW II 1941-45
RONALD L.	BESKE	ARMY ENGINEER	1963-66
BRIAN C.	BESKE	ARMY AMMO S/4	ARBN 1975-79
RICHARD A.	BESKE	ARMY AIRBORNE	VIETNAM 1968-85
LEONARD	BESKE	COAST GUARD GMI	WW II 1942-46
JOHN D.	BEULE	ARMY AIR CORP	WW II 1942-46
BURTON H.	BEYER	ARMY PFC	KOREA-1951-53
WARREN L.	BEYER	NAVY S/1 CARRIER	WW II
HAROLD P.	BIEL	ARMY STAFF SGT	WW II
EUGENE	BILKE	NAVY SEABEES	WW II 1945-47
TERRY A.	BILKE	NAVY EM/1 & NG MAJ	1973-1997
EDWIN R.	BILKE	ARMY 1ST/SGT	WIA WW I 1917-18
NORMAN W.	BILKE	NAVY F 1/C ESCORT	PACIFIC WW II
RALPH W.	BILL	PERCIFIELD	ARMY WW II
HARVEY W.	BINDER	ARMY MEDICAL CORP	WW II 1943-46
EDWARD J.	BISLEW	AF BOMBER GUNNER	DIED-POW-JAPAN-WW II
EUGENE L.	BITTNER	ARMY MP CPL.	JAPAN 1952-54
DAWN	BLANCHARD	ARMY CWO	1979-CAREER
BILL	BLANCHARD	ARMY CSM	1974-CAREER
JIM	BLOOMFIELD	ARMY	1966-1968
ELMER E.	BOBHOLZ	ARMY INF.	FRANCE WW I
ALVIN J.	BONACK	ARMY INTERPRETER	WW II 1944-46
DONALD	BOOTH	COAST GUARD SIC/R	WW II 1942-45
ROBERT W.	BORTH	ARMY PVT.	WW II
W. E.	BOUSHON	ARMY	S. PACIFIC WW II
R. W.	BRADLEY SR.	ARMY CPL.	WW II
GEORGE B.	BRAUN	ARMY INF. PVT.	DEPOT BR. 1917-18
ROLAND	BRAUN	AAF GUNNER B 25	KIA WW II 1942
RALPH A.	BRAUN	ARMY TANK CPL	WW II 1943-46
ELDEN A.	BRAUN	ARMY HQS TROOPS	JAPAN 1954-56

DWAYNE A.	BRAUN	ARMY	1952-54
GERALD W.	BRAUN	ARMY S/SGT	KOREA-1969-71
ROBERT R.	BRAUN	ARMY INFANTRY	VIETNAM 1967-1969
DENNIS L.	BRAUN	ARMY	GERMANY 1962-65
JAMES R.	BRAUN	USAR COOK	1962-68
KENNETH	BRAUN	ARMY HONOR GUARD	WASHINGTON D. C.
HARRY H.	BRAUN JR.	NAVY COOK	PACIFIC-WW II
AUG.	BRAUNSCHWEIG	ARMY CPL.	EUROPE WW II
G. C.	BREITKREUTZ	NAVY CORAL SEA	1965-67
R. A.	BREITKREUTZ	ARMY INF. SGT.	1964-66
ORVILLE	BREMER	ARMY MECHANIC	WW II 1942-45
GARY LEE	BREMER	ARMY INFANTRY	VIETNAM 1967-69
HARVEY C.	BREMER	AIR FORCE SGT	EUROPE WW II
BERNARD	BREUER	ARMY 40TH ENG.	WIA-WW II
TROY A.	BREWER	ARMY	GERMANY 1986-89
MATTHEW	BREWER	MARINE	GULF WAR I 1989-93
PATRICK	BREWER	ARMY ARNG	1997-98
GEO.	BROMBEREK	967TH ARTILLERY	UNKNOWN
GILBERT	BROOKS	ARMY RADIO COM.	T/4 WW II 1942-44
LARRY A.	BROOKS	ARMY MAINT.	VIETNAM
LEROY W.	BROOME	ARMY SIG. CORP E/6	WIA WW II
DAVID L.	BROOME	NAVY SEABEES	1956-60
GARY J.	BROOME	ARMY GUN CHIEF SGT.	WIA VIETNAM 1970
ROBERT H.	BROWER	SIGNAL CORP	WW II 1939-45
R PETER	BROWER	NAVY	1967-73
STILMAN E.	BROWN	ARMY CORPORAL	ETO D-DAY WW II
EDGAR S.	BROWN	ARMY T/SGT	32ND DIVISION WW II
DOUGLAS	BROWN	ARMY MEDIC	EUROPE WW II
LESTER	BROWN	ARMY NG 1/SGT.	KIA PACIFIC WW II
CHESTER A.	BROWN	ARMY ENGINEER	WW I
WAYNE	BRUESSEL	NAVY HANK 702	1955-57
JAMES A.	BUBLITZ	ARMY SP/5	1972-75
ROBERT	BUCHDA	ARMY AIR FORCE	WW II
AL J	BUDDE	NAVY RM/3	1954-56
ROBERT J.	BUDDE	ARMY SFC ARMOR	KOREA-1951-1952
GORDON	BURBACH	ARMY CPL	1952-54
ALVIN W.	BURBACH	NAVY	PACIFIC-WW II
SAM	BURCHARD	BEAVER DAM 1880	BURCHARD GUARD
ALEX	BURCHARDT	NAVY USS BELL	WW II 1943-45
ALVIN	BURGDORFF	ARMY INFANTRY	WW I
JERRY L.	BUSCHKE	AIR FORCE	KOREA 1951-54
ALLEN H.	BUSKE	ARMY 32ND DIV.	WW II 1940-45
VICTOR W.	BUSS	8TH ARMY 720TH MP	TOKYO 1945-46
ALFRED	BUSS	NAVY DESTROYER	KIA OKINAWA WW II
ALBERT L.	BUSS	USAF FLT. LINE	KOREA
JULIAN A.	BUSS	MARINE 6TH DIV.	PACIFIC-1942-45
EDWARD J.	BUSS	ARMY ENGINEER SGT	KOREA-1952-1953
J. E.	BUSSEWITZ	NAVY EM/3	1951-54
JOHN	BUTTERBRODT	USMC S/SGT	KOREA
GILBERT	CALLIES	NAVY F 1/C	WW II 1943-46
W. "BILL"	CALLIES	COAST GUARD	OP DEEP FREEZE

GLENN A.	CALLIES	NAVY SUBMARINER	VIETNAM 1971-77
RONALD	CALLIES	ARMY ENGINEER	FRANCE 1954-56
DEL	CAMPNELL JR.	ARMY CPL.	KOREA
TRACY H.	CANNIFF	ARMY SPECIALIST	VIETNAM 1964-66
RYAN J.	CANTAFIO	MARINE	KIA IRAQ 11/26/2004
CASEY O.	CARNEY	NAVY SONAR TECH.	1975-81
ERVIN	CASSABAUM	ARMY TK DRIVER	WW II 1944-45
SANDRA	CASTILLO	US ARMY	1982-91
ROBERT W.	CAUGHLIN	AIR FORCE A/2C	VIETNAM 1962-66
RAY W.	CAUGHLIN	ARMY AIR CORP	CPL. WW II 1942-45
MIKE	CHAMBERLAIN	ARMY INFANTRY	VIETNAM-1967-68
EARNEST J.	CHARON	ARMY SIGNAL BN.	FRANCE WW I
FRANK J.	CHATHAM	ARMY POST OFFICE	WW II
ED.	CHRISTIAN	ARMY WACOM	GERMANY-1953-55
DICK	CIGELSKE	MARINE 4TH DIV.	1963-69
BOB	CIGELSKE	MARINE 4TH DIV.	1963-69
CLARENCE A.	CIGELSKE	ARMY S/SERGEANT	WW II-1941-45
GORDON A.	CISCO	MARINE CPL	PACIFIC-WW II
RAYMOND A.	CLARK	NAVY SEAMAN 1/C	WW I 1917-19
JOHN A.	CLARK SR.	ARMY T/5 89TH DIV.	EUROPE WW II
PAUL V.	CLOYD	NAVY	1945-1946
MONCURE	COLEMAN	AIR FORCE GUNNER	ETO WW II
JOSEPH C.	COLEMAN	ARMY PFC AAA BN	ITALY-WW II
WARREN C.	COLEMAN	ARMY INF MAJOR	W.I.A. WW II-1940-1962
JACK L.	COLEMAN	ARMY ARTILLERY	EUROPE-WW II
F. "BILL"	CONNORS	NAVY LIEUTENANT	1943-46 1952-54
WM.	COXSHALL	ARMY HANGMAN	CIVIL WAR
CHRIS	CRANDALL	MARINE RADIO OP.	GULF WAR II
R.	CRANDALL JR.	MARINE CORPORAL	GULF WAR I
R.	CRANDALL SR.	NAVY FBM SUBS	VIETNAM
EBENEZER A.	CRANE	ARMY CO.D 5TH WIS	CIVIL WAR-1864-65
FRANK H.	CRANE	ARMY COMMISSARY	SPANISH-AMER. WAR
CHARLES W.	CRANE	ARMY 32D DIVISION	EUROPE-WW II
RUSSELL W.	CRANE	ARMY 62D MAINT BN	VIETNAM-!965-69
GEORGE M.	CRANE	ARMY W.I.A.	SOUTH PACIFIC-WW II
BUEHL H.	CUFF	NAVY ARMED GUARD	WW II 1943-46
CLARENCE	CULLEN	NAVY S I/C	WW II 1945-46
CLARENCE	CULLEN	NAVY MM/2 USNRF	FRANCE WW I
R. J.	CUNNINGHAM	ARMY	FRANCE WW I
JOHN	CUNNINGHAM	ARMY ORDNANCE	FRANCE WW I
E. A.	CUNNINGHAM	ARMY	WW I & WWII
E. "SARG"	CZARNESKI	ARMY AIR FORCE	WW II 1944-46
ORVILLE F.	DAHL	ARMY MEDIC	PACIFIC WW II
WILLIAM R.	DAVIS	MARINE GY SGT	VIETNAM
THAYER	DAVIS	ARMY DOCTOR	KOREAN WAR
RON. C.	DAVISON	ARMY ENGINEER	VIETNAM 1968-69
EUGENE	DE YOUNG	NAVY ENSIGN	WW II
MILO F.	DEGLOW	NAVY MOMM 2/C	WW II 1943-45
FRED	DEIBERT	ARMY 199TH INF BDE	VIETNAM 1968-70
PETER	DEMMERLE	NAVY-COASTGUARD	1957-72
RALPH	DESJARLAIS	NAVY GUARD	KOREA 1951-54

WALTER E.	DEWITZ	ARMY T/4	WW II 1940-45
DELBERT	DEYOUNG	MARINE CORPORAL	WW II
TALMAGE	DIEK	DIEKVOSS	ARMY KOREA
JOE	DIESLER JR.	AIR FORCE SGT	KOREA 1950-1954
DALE L.	DINKEL	ARMY AUSARTY	1955-59
DONALD	DINKEL	COAST GUARD 2/C	WW II
WERNER A.	DINKEL	ARMY CORPORAL	GERMANY 1951-53
DON J.	DOHMANN	8TH A. F. S/SGT	ENGLAND-WW II 43-46
ALBERT C.	DOLLAR	317 MACH. GUN BTN	WW I
DOUGLAS	DOLLAR	AIR POLICEMAN	1951-55
CALVIN T.	DOLLAR	AAF B17 CREW	EUROPE-WW II
CARL A.	DOLLAR	ARMY INFANTRY	ITALY—WW II
DONALD D.	DORN	ARMY INFANTRY	COLD WAR 1954-56
GORDON L.	DORN	ARMY INFANTRY	1952-1973
GLENN R.	DORN	AIR CORP T/SGT	WW II-1941-46
DUDLEY D.	DORN	NAVY RM 1/C	1942-1948
THOMAS J.	DOVER	1ST CAV S/SGT	KOREA
STANLEY	DRAHEIM	ARMY CPL.	WW II
GEORGE	DRAHEIM	WIS. NAT GUARD 1/LT	WIA WWI 1905-1919
RUSSELL H	DRAKE	AIR FORCE	JAPAN 1949-52
IRVIN C.	DRUCKREY	ARMY	1944-45
RUSS H.	DRUECKE	AIR FORCE T/SGT	WW II
SCOTT R.	DRUECKE	AIR FORCE A 1/C	WW II
DONALD	DUERST	ARMY ARTILLERY	KOREA 1946-48
C. L.	DUESSLER	ARMY	WW II
DAVID E.	DUMMER	AIR FORCE	1964-1968
WILLIAM G.	DUMMER	ARMY 3RD ARMOR	GERMANY-1951-52
ARVEL J.	DUNCAN	ARMY SGT	WIA EUROPE WW II
EARL E.	DUSELL	ARMY SERGEANT	WW II
HERB.	DUZINSKI	ARMY	WW I-1915-17
BERNARD J.	DYLAK	ARMY ENGINEER	WW II
NATHAN J.	EBERT	NAVY EM/2 CV 60	GULF WAR I
LAVERN F.	EBERT	AIR FORCE S/SGT	940TH LOADMASTER
BERTHOLD H.	EBERT	ARMY ARTILLERY	PVT-WW I
JAMES L.	EBERT	82ND AIRBORNE	PANAMA & IRAQ
VINCENT H.	EBERT	ARMY MEDIC	EUROPE WW II
DELMAR F.	EBERT	ARMY COOK CPL.	JAPAN & KOREA
RONALD J.	EBERT	NAVY AIR FORCE	KOREA 1951-55
ELEANOR	EDWARDS	ARMY NURSE CAPT.	CBI WW II
ROBERT	EDWARDS	ARMY COLONEL	CBI WW II
MORRIS L.	EGGERT	AIR FORCE MECH.	KOREA
BOB	EHLENFELDT	ARMY SP/5	VIETNAM 1969-72
CHAS.	EHLENFELDT	COAST GUARD YN/3	1954-58
R. "RED"	EHLENFELDT	NAVY DD532	PACIFIC WWII
ROY W.	EHLERT	ARMY	WW II 1943-1946
ROWLAND W	EICHEL	ARMY CORPORAL	FRANCE WW I
COL. T. F.	EICHEL	ARMY DENTAL CORP	KOREA & CAREER
JACK R.	EICHEL	NAVY CARRIER	WW II & KOREA
THOMAS A	EILBES	ARMY SP/5	1968-71
FRANK	ELEGREET	ARMY SGT.	WW II 1942-45
WARD A.	ELLIOTT	ARMY SGT.	WW II 1944-46

ELDEN R.	ELSESSER	NAVY GUNNER	PACIFIC WW II
WM. "BILL"	EMANUEL	NAVY BATTLESHIP	LIEUTENANT-WW II
ERVE	ENDTHOFF	ARMY CPL	MEXICAN BORDER
HERBIE	ENDTHOFF	ARMY 24TH INF. PFC	WW II
F. E.	ENGEBRETSON	ARMY ORDNANCE	PACIFIC-WW II-1944-46
WALTER H.	ERBER	ARMY RESERVES	1953-59
RICHARD	ERDMAN	MARINE CPL.	1956-64
DUANE R.	FANSHAW	NAVY MP & BAKER	KOREA-1951-55
HARVEY	FEHLING	US NAVY CPO	WW II 1939-45
JOHN	FEHLING	ARMY TANK BN	KOREA 1950-52
CHRIST.	FEHLING	ARMY CO.K 53RD INF	FRANCE WW I 1918
ROBERT C.	FEHRMAN	ARMY ENGINEERS	KOREA
BILL R.	FERRIES	ARMY 1ST SCOUT	ITALY WW II
MICHAEL	FERRON	ARMY SP/4	VIETNAM 1967-70
JAMES F.	FERRON	ARMY INFANTRY T/5	ETO WW II 1942-45
MICHAEL	FERSTL	ARMY PFC.	VIETNAM 1967-69
CLARENCE	FERSTL	ARMY PFC.	WW II 1942-45
DANIEL	FEULING	ARMY NG LTC	26 YEARS 1970-96
DAVID T.	FEULING	ARMY SPEC. 5	VIETNAM
THOMAS J.	FEULING	ARMY TEC 5	WW II
ROBERT	FIEBELKORN	ARMY 10TH MTN DIV.	ITALY WWII
HAROLD A.	FIEGEL	ARMY ARTILLERY	ETO-WW II-1942-46
DAVID W.	FIERKE	ARMY ARTILLERY	LT. COL. 1941-45
RAYMOND	FIRARI	ARMY INFANTRY	WW II 1945-46
WALLY	FISCHBACH	MERCHANT MARINE	POW GERMANY WW II
BRETT M.	FISCHER	ARMY SFC AMMO	DESERT STORM
CHAS. R.	FISHER	ARMY ENGINEER	CAPT. EUROPE WW I
A. R.	FITZSIMMONS	ARMY 1ST LT.	WW II NURSE PACIFIC
ELAINE	FLAHERTY	ARMY AIR CORP (WAC)	WW II 1944-45
ELWOOD	FLAHERTY	ARMY AIR CORP	WW II 1943-46
JAMES	FLETCHER	AIR CORP SGT	FLT. ENG. 1942-45
LLOYD E.	FRANK	ARMY T/5 MEDIC	ETO WW II 1942-45
MILTON W.	FRANK	ARMY T/5 TANK	WIA WW II 1942-46
DELMAR A.	FRANK	ARMY INF. PVT	KIA WW II 1943
GORDON W.	FRANK	NAVY BOMBARDIER	N. PACIFIC-1942-46
ARTHUR H.	FRANK	ARMY 331ST FA	CPL. FRANCE WW I
JEROME A.	FRANK	MORTAR MAN PFC	JAPAN 1946-48
ARTHUR R.	FRANK	ARMY MEDIC PVT	ITALY 1949-51
VICTOR	FRANKE	ARMY	WW II
ELSMER	FRANKE	ARMY S/SGT	K.I.A. WW II
ALAN	FRANKE	MARINE CPL.	KOREA
ROBERT H	FRANKENSTEIN	ARMY ENGINEER	KOREA
DICK J.	FREDERICK	ARMY AIR CORP IG	WW II 1942-46
PETER J.	FREITAG	AIR FORCE MECH.	ICELAND 1959-63
HARRY F.	FRIESE	ARMY MEDIC	WW I
WAYNE	FRIESE	ARMY	1963-65
JUDY K.	FRIESE	ARMY POL	1980-84
FRED C.	FRIESE	ARMY SIGNAL CORP.	KOREA 1953-55
FRED	FRIESE JR.	NAVY CARRIER	VIETNAM 1974-76
DR. WM.	FUNCKE	NAVY RADAR TECH.	WW II 1945-46
KENNETH O.	GADE	ARMY	WW II

DONALD	GAHLMAN	ARMY SIGNAL CORP.	KOREA 1950-51
ROB'T	GAHLMAN	MARINE SGT. 4TH REG.	K.I.A. IWO JIMA WW II
WILLIAM	GAHLMAN	AIR FORCE CPL.	GUAM WW II
LON P.	GAMBLE	MARINE CPL	1979-83
JOHN	GARCZYNSKI	NAVY CM/3	PACIFIC-WW II
ROBERT J.	GARTZKE	US NAVY	WW II
ELWOOD J.	GARVIN	ARMY SKYWARF	KOREA
KENNETH	GEDAMKE	USAF A 2/C CLERK	KOREA 1951-53
MERLIN G.	GENTZ	ARMY SERGEANT	BERLIN CRISIS-1961-62
PHILIP J.	GERG	ARMY AIR CORP	WW II
PHILIP L.	GERG	AIR FORCE M/SGT.	VIETNAM 1963-84
PEGGY A.	GERG	AIR FORCE S/SGT	1978-82
DALE J.	GERKE	MARINES S/SGT	KOREA 1954-57
GERALD	GERKE	ARMY SP/3	KOREA 1954-56
RICHARD H	GIESE	NAVY TMC	1953-73
BILL	GIESE	ARMY SGT.	WW II
CLARENCE	GIESE	ARMY 95TH INF. S/SGT.	WIA FRANCE WW II
LINDA K.	GIESE	ARMY SP/5	1972-76
WILLIAM	GIESE	NAVY SF/3	WW II 1942-45
ARDEN	GIESE	MARINE 1942-45	WIA. PACIFIC WW II
MICHAEL	GIESE	NAVY 2/C	VIETNAM 1966-68
LESTER G.	GIESE	ARMY ENGINEER	WW II-KOREA
WILBERT W.	GIESE	ARMY TECH 4	WW II
DELMAR A.	GIESE	NAVY USS RENO	BM 2/C-1942-1945
HILBERT	GIETZEL	ARMY 1ST/SGT	EUROPE WW II
ERVIN H.	GILHART	ARMY SP/4	GERMANY 1958-60
ROBERT	GILMORE	ARMY-NAVY CM/1	SAIPAN WW II
DON. J.	GOCKER	NAVY RADARMAN	1945-48
PETER C.	GOCKER	ARMY SP/5	VIETNAM 1966-69
LEO L	GOCKER	ARMY—COLONEL	WWI—WW II
DONALD	GOELLER	ARMY SIGNAL CORP	
THERESA	GOELLER	ARMY MP	IRAQ 2003
HARVEY	GOETSCH	ARMY CPL	KOREA-1952-54
ROBERT	GOETSCH	ARMY SIGNAL CORP	1954-1955
RALPH.	GOETTING SR	AIR FORCE PILOT	CBI-WW II
DANIEL G.	GOETZ	ARMY	1943-1946
D. "BUGS"	GOODRICH	ARMY ENGINEERS	KOREA 1953-55
C. KELLY	GOODRICH	MARINE PVT	CP PENDLETON, CA
ROBERT	GOODWIN	AIR FORCE 2/LT.	WW II 1943-47
LYLE C.	GOSSFELD	ARMY 357TH INF.	WW II 1944-45
CARROLL L.	GOVE	USS INDIANAPOLIS	KIA PACIFIC WW II
RAYMOND	GRADEL	ARMY INFANTRY	WW II 1940-45
RUSSELL	GRADEL	USAF LT. COLONEL	WW II 1941-1963
NORMAN W.	GRAHN	NAVY TE/1	1953-57
BRUCE A.	GRAHN	NAVY RM 2/C	1977-1981
R. J.	GRAINER JR.	ARMY TANK CORP.	POW GERMANY WW II
MARK H.	GRAMS	MARINE GYSGT	1974-81 & 1982-95
JAMES L.	GRANT	ARMY TANK SGT	WW II 1943-1945
RICHARD	GRAPER	ARMY FOOD INSPEC	FRANCE-1954-56
RUBEN	GREENFIELD	ARMY HELO MECH.	CPL. KOREA 1952-54
EUGENE	GREINER	ARMY TANK SGT	ETO-WW II 1942-45

GLEN E.	GREINKE	MARINE 4TH DIV.	PACIFIC-WW II
ART.	GRIEBENOW	ARMY ENGINEER	EUROPE-WW II
GORDON	GRIESBACH	PFC 358 INF 90TH DIV.	KIA JULY 23, 1944
JAMES	GRIESBACH	384 FIGHTER SQ. SGT	WW II 1942-45
D.	GRIESBACH	721ST ARTILLERY	ETO WW II 1944-46
ROSEANN	GROB	ARMY MEDIC MAJOR	DESERT STORM & 9-11
ARMIN	GROSENICK	USN MINESWEEPER	WW II
REYNOLD	GUENTHER	ARMY SGT	KOREA 1953-54
DORIS E.	GUSE	ARMY WAC PFC	WW II
PERCY A.	GUSE	ARMY MEDICAL CLK	FRANCE-WW I
ROGER A.	GUSE	ARMY PFC	K.I.A.-ITALY-WW II
ROBERT A.	GUSE	ARMY MECHANIC	1965-1967
DUANE B.	HAAS	AIR FORCE S/SGT.	WW II
JAMES E.	HAASE	NAVY SEAMAN 1/C	WW II 1943-46
RALPH W.	HAASE	NAVY MIDWAY	AIRMAN 1948-53
JEROME A.	HAASE	MARINE	1951
STEVEN H.	HAASE	ARMY SPEC/4	VIETNAM
LES.	HAFENSTEIN	COAST GUARD/NAVY	WW II 1942-45
HERB	HAFENSTEIN	NAVY 2ND MATE	WW II 1942-45
TERRY L	HAMMER	AIR FORCE	1963-1967
ERVIN F.	HAMMER	ARMY	1943-45
THOMAS	HAMMER	ARMY	KOREA
JOSEPH J.	HANKES	AIR FORCE PILOT	CBI-WW II 1941-46
EDWARD A.	HANKES	MARINE S/SGT	OKINAWA-WW II 1943-45
ROBERT J.	HANKES	ARMY 25TH INF.	VIETNAM
JACK	HANKES	AIR FORCE S/SGT.	1971-79
ALFRED P.	HANKES	COAST GUARD	CARPENTER WW II
T. CHRIST	HANSEN	ARMY ENGINEER	WW I
REYNOLD	HANSEN	U. S. ARMY	WW I
MARK B.	HANSEN	ARMY ARTILLERY	S. PHILIPPINES-WWII
ROBERT H.	HANSER	ARMY CPL.	WW II 1941-46
EDWARD G.	HARDER	ARMY ARTILLERY	EUROPE WW II
MICHAEL	HARMSEN	MARINE INTEL.	VIETNAM
MICHAEL A.	HARTL	AIR FORCE	1952-1956
ROBERT	HARTMAN	NAVY SEABEE LT.	SO. PACIFIC WW II
FRANK A.	HARTWIG	ARMY GUNNER SGT	WW II 1942-46
JOHN	HARTZHEIM	AIR FORCE S/SGT	PACIFIC-WW II
PAUL	HARTZHEIM	ARMY S/SGT 88 DIV	KIA-ITALY-WW II
LARRY	HASENSTAB	MARINE CPL.	VIETNAM 1959-63
LYNN	HASENSTAB	A.F. SGT. MISSILE SQD.	LAFB VA. 1965-69
H. J.	HATZINGER	ARMY T/SGT	WW II 1941-45
JOHN	HATZINGER	ARMY SP/5	1967-70
URBAN	HATZINGER	ARMY AIR FORCE	1942-45
WAYNE	HAWKINS	ARMY SP/4	VIETNAM 1966-68
NICHOLAS	HEIDT	AIR FORCE SGT	PACIFIC-WW II
ELMER	HEIMERL	ARMY ARTILLERY	1942-45
ARTHUR G.	HEIMLER	ARMY T/3	WW II
HAROLD	HEINEMEIER	ARMY MP	WW II 1942-45
KENNETH H.	HEINTZ	ARMY SGT	WW II
HOWARD	HELBING	US NAVY SCB/2	WW II 1945-46
GERHARDT	HELING	ARMY CORPORAL	WW I 1915-1919

TOM C.	HELMBRECHT	ARMY NAVY LT. DDS	WW II & KOREA
KENNETH	HELMER	MARINE CPL.	KOREA 1951-53
ART. E.	HELMER SR.	MARINE CPL	WW II 1944-46
FLOYD R.	HENSCHEL	NAVY TEL 3	ITALY-1952-55
VICTOR A.	HERBST	ARMY 554TH ENG.	CORP HQ 1957-60
JOE. F.	HERMAN SR.	MARINE CPL.	KOREA
EARL A.	HERREMAN	ARMY GERMANY	WW II 1942-45
THOMAS J.	HICKEY	MARINE S/SGT.	SO. PACIFIC WW II
GEORGE L.	HICKEY	NAVY SEABEES 2/C	SO. PACIFIC WW II
JAMES	HICKEY	MARINE CPL.	CBI 1946-48
LEONARD	HICKEY	AIR FORCE S/SGT.	JAPAN 1952-54
DONALD E.	HILEY	ARMY SWITCHBOARD	GERMANY 1953-55
LLOYD	HILEY SR	ARMY SGT	KOREA
C. W.	HILGENDORF	ARMY AIR CORP.	K.I.A. PAMAMA WW II
JOHN D.	HILL	NAVY GM MTB	PACIFIC-WW II
RODNEY H.	HILL	ARMY SP/4	1980-86
EDMUND J.	HINKES	ARMY PVT.	WW I
SILVERIUS	HINKES	NAVY & ARMY	WW II & KOREA
MERLIN E.	HINKES	NAVY USS LIBRA 12	1952-56
CLYDE V.	HODGSON	ARMY INFANTRY	KOREA
DICK	HOEFS	AIR FORCE CAPT.	1951-53
WM. J.	HOEFS JR.	USAAF WEATHER	CHINA BURMA WW II
WM. J.	HOEFS SR.	AES	FRANCE WW I
KENNETH	HOEHNE	ARMY	VIETNAM
ROBERT J.	HOEVET	USN PC-1077 QM 1/C	PACIFIC WW II
ANTHONY	HOFFMAN	ARMY 31ST INF.	PHILIPPINES WW II
FRANCIS	HOFFMAN	8TH AIR FORCE	ENGLAND WW II
BILL	HOLLIHAN	ARMY	PANAMA
DONALD	HOLLNAGEL	ARMY	WW II 1941-1945
WILLIAM J.	HOMAN	MARINE MP PFC	IWO JIMA WW II
ALVIN C.	HOPPE	MARINE	1957-60
DAVID W.	HORGAN	ARMY	PACIFIC-WW II
DON R.	HOWLAND	ARMY	WW II-1944-1947
CHARLES R.	HRON	ARMY INFANTRY	1947-1950 KOREA
RONALD E.	HRON	ARMY HELO MECH.	SP/4 1977-80
ROBERT C.	HRON	US MARINE CORP	1977-1981
CHARLES	HUETTL	NAVY GATOR FLT	SANDIEGO 196-64
DAVID L.	HUPF	NAVY BMC E/7	1968-1993
JEROME J.	HUPF	A. F. WEATHERMAN	ICELAND WW II 1945-46
DALE J.	HUPF	NAVY	1971-74
DOUGLAS F.	HUPF	ARMY INTELLIGENCE	1977-97
DEAN P.	HUPF	MARINES	1974-75
THOMAS G.	HUPF	ARMY MAILMAN	KOREA
DENNIS J.	HUPF	ARMY ENGINEER E/5	VIETNAM-1965-67
MICHAEL	HUSSLI	AIR FORCE CAREER	WW II-KOREA
KARL G.	HUTTER	ARMY CAPTAIN	EUROPE-WW II
ALBERT J.	HUTTER	NAVY SEABEES	PACIFIC 1943-46
CHARLIE	HUTTER	NAVY USS ORISKANY	VIETNAM1969-73
THOMAS W.	HYDE	ARMY TANK 10TH MTN	EUROPE-1955-57
JAMES	ILLINGWORTH	ARMY 104TH INF. DIV.	KIA WW II
WARREN F.	IMME	NAVY SEAMAN 1/C	WW II 1945-46

LLOYD	IMMERFALL	ARMY INF. PFC.	1951-1953
"BUTCH"	IMMERFALL	ARMY ARTILLERY	WW II
JR. F.	IMMERFALL	ARMY SERGEANT	7TH CAVALRY-KOREA
LLOYD R.	IPSEN	ARMY MEDIC	KOREA 1952-54
C. J.	JACKMAN	ARMY 2ND DIVISION	ETO-WW II 1942-45
DONALD R.	JACOB	AIR FORCE S/SGT	1951-55
RODEL J.	JACOB	ARMY	WW I
ROBERT C.	JACOB	ARMY A. A.	IWO JIMA WW II
EDWARD H.	JACOBS	AMERICAN EXPED.	WW I 1917-18
EDWARD M.	JACOBS	ARMY AIR CORP.	SGT. 1942-46
R. F.	JACOBS	G/2 10TH MTN DIV.	WW II 1942-46
MICHAEL	JACOBS	1ST LT. JAG	AIR CORP WW II
JOHN R.	JACOBS	1ST ARMORED DIV.	CAPT. WW II-KOREA
FRED	JACOBS	ARMY S/SGT	WW II
LYLE W	JAEHNKE	ARMY ENG SGT	1953-54
S.WOLC	JAEHNKE	W/MARINE PFC	1956-57
WM C.	JAEHNKE	ARMY PFC	WW I
EDGAR	JAEHNKE	ARMY TANKER T/5	ETO WW II
"BUD" R.	JAHNCKE	MERCHANT MARINE	WW II-1943-45
FRANK S.	JANCZAK	AF PILOT TRAINER	ETO & CBI WW II
JOHN J.	JANCZAK	AF PILOT TRAINER	RESERVES WW II
PETER W.	JANZ	ARMY	PACIFIC WW II
RONALD J.	JENKINS	ARMY CPL.	1951-52
ALOIS	JEZYK	ARMY SGT.	WW II 1942-45
RANDAL H.	JOECKEL	ARMY CWO	KUWAIT 2004-05
THOMAS	JOHNSON	COAST GUARD CDR	GULF WAR I 1968-95
REV. T.S.	JOHNSON	CHAPLAIN	CIVIL WAR
EARL D.	JOHNSON	MEDICAL CORP	WW I 1918
WM.	JOHNSON	ARMY AIRBORNE	KOREA
LESLIE W.	JONES	ARMY STAFF SGT.	INF. ITALY WW II
JOHN	KACZMARSKI	AAF CORPORAL	WW II 1941-45
JAMES F.	KAISER	US NAVY	WW II 1944-46
RUBEN J.	KAISER	AIR FORCE PILOT	1ST/LT. ITALY WW II
DICK	KAISER	ARMY S/SGT	KOREA-1951-1953
MELVIN	KAMRATH	AAF S/SGT.	WW II 1942-45
LT. COL. ORVAL	KANE	AF BOMBER PILOT	S. W. PACIFIC-WW II
EUGENE F	KARL	ARMY INF SGT	WWII—BERLIN CRISIS
HAROLD B.	KARL	MARAUDERS T/5	WW II
EDWIN W.	KARST	ARMY ENGINEER	SGT.-KIA-WW II
BOB	KASTENMEIER	ARMY INF. 1/LT.	PACIFIC WW II 1943-46
J. C.	KASTENMEIER	COMBAT ENGINEER	CBI-WW II
ELTON F.	KAUL	ARMY SGT.	KOREA
HARVEY J.	KAUL	ARMY SGT.	WW I
ROY S.	KEITH	MARINE	WW II 1942-46
DAVID S.	KEITH	MARINE	VIETNAM 1968-72
HAROLD F.	KEMPFER	AIR FORCE	1951-53
EUGENE	KENITZER	ARMY INFANTRY	SERGEANT-1952-54
NORMAN R.	KENNING	AAF ORDNANCE TEC.	WW II
LESTER A.	KENNING	NAVY YN/3	WW II & KOREA
LAWRENCE	KENNING	NAVY SN	KOREA
CLARENCE	KESKE	ARMY DSC PH BS	KIA FRANCE WW I

CLARENCE J.	KESKE	ARMY DEMOLITION	PFC. ETO WW II
MERLIN A.	KEYSER	ARMY AIR FORCE	WW II
WM. B.	KIEKHAEFER	ARMY MI	VIETNAM 1969-71
FRANK	KIEKHAEFER SR.	ARMY SIGNAL CORP	1953-55
ELWOOD J.	KIEL	ARMY CORPORAL	WW II-1943-1945
JOHN F.	KIENOW	NAVY KITTY HAWK	1959-63
CHARLES A.	KING	ARMY RADAR SGT.	PACIFIC WW II
LEROY	KIRCHBERG	MERCHANT MARINE	WW II 1943-47
JOHN	KIRCHBERG	ARMY S/5	VIETNAM
GLEN	KIRCHBERG	PARATROOPER	WW II 1941-45
ROBERT	KIRCHOFF	US NAVY	LOST AT SEA-1958
GERALD	KIRSCHKE	A. F. NAVIGATOR	P.O.W.-EUROPE-WW II
FRANK A.	KIRSCHT	ARMY MEDIC	FRANCE WW II
FRANCIS	KIRSCHT	ARMY ARTILLERY	EUROPE 1944-46
HUGH L.	KIRSH	AIR FORCE M/SGT.	CBI-WW II 1943-45
JAMES	KIRSH SR.	NAVY	WW II
CLARENCE	KISER	AF MECHANIC S/SGT	KOREA 1949-52
GLEN R.	KJORNES	ARMY 4TH DIV.	VIETNAM 1967-69
GERALD	KJORNES	ARMY GULF WAR	PROUD TO SERVE
CHRISTY	KJORNES	USAF CREW CHIEF	WAR ON TERROR
BOB	KLARKOWSKI	ARMY INF. GUNNER	PACIFIC WW II 1942-46
ELLERY A.	KLATT	ARMY INFANTRY	GERMANY WW II
AL. A.	KLAVEKOSKE	NAVY REPAIR SHIP	WW II—KOREA
RICH	KLAVEKOSKE	ARMY CORPORAL	KOREAN CONFLICT
DON	KLAVEKOSKE	NAVY USS MIDWAY	1956-59
MARV.	KLAWITTER	ARMY CORPORAL	KOREA 1950-52
ROGER	KLAWITTER	ARMY	KOREA 1952-53
JACK	KLEIN	ARMY CIA	CHINA WW II
LAWRENCE	KLEINDL	US ARMY	WW II
DAVID	KLEINDL	ARMY CORPORAL	1953-1955
W. F.	KLEINDL JR.	11TH AIRBORNE	JAPAN-1946-47
KEITH D.	KLINE	ARMY PARATROOPER	1947-51 KOREAN WAR
LEON	KLINGER	NAVY E/5 PC	VIETNAM-1968-72
EARL	KLOSSNER	ARMY SGT/MAJOR	1945-76
DANIEL	KLOSSNER	ARMY MEDIC	25TH INF—VIETNAM
ROGER S.	KLUG	MARINE GRUNT	VIETNAM-1969-71
LEROY L.	KLUG	AIR FORCE S/SGT	WW II 1942-45
EARL A.	KLUG	ARMY	EUROPE WW II
ERVIN E.	KLUG	AIR FORCE S/SGT.	EUROPE-WW II
STANLEY H.	KNAAK	NAVY	PACIFIC WW II
ORIN J	KNOLL	ARMY AIR CORP	WW II
ROLAND B.	KNORR	ARMY SURG TECH.	1942-45
ROBERT	KOCH	ARMY RESERVES	AAA 1958-65
KEN E.	KOERNER	USAF FLIGHT ENG.	JAPAN-KOREA 1952-56
WILBERT	KOERNER	ARMY INFANTRY	WIA ETO. WW II 1943-45
ROLAND W.	KOERNER	US ARMY SGT	KOREA-1952-54
TIMOTHY	KOHL	WIS AIR GUARD	M/SGT. 1983-2003
DELMAR G.	KOHL	AIR FORCE	1952-56
MERLIN J.	KOHL	ARMY ENGINEER	KOREA 1953-54
ALLAN A.	KOHLS	ARMY MEDIC	VIETNAM 1969-71
HARVEY D.	KOHLS	ARMY CHAUFFEUR	1960-62

DENNIS J.	KOHN	ARMY SGT.	PAMAMA 1968-70
DUANE D.	KOLB	MARINE L/CPL.	1977-80
EUGENE R.	KOLB	NAVY	WW II 1941-43
ANDREW	KOLB	ARMY	WW I
HARVEY J.	KOPFF	AAF RADIO OP.	WW II 1943-46
CAPT. DAN	KORDUS	B26 PILOT ETO WW II	WIS. NAT.GUARD.-RET.
AMBROSE B.	KORES	ARMY MEDIC MAJOR	ETO WW II 1942-46
L. BEVERLY	KORES	ARMY NURSE CAPT.	ETO WW II 1944-46
WILTON	KORTH	ARMY MECHANIC	ETO WW II 1942-45
CALVIN F.	KORTH	A.F. AIRCRAFT ELECT	POPE AFB 1955-58
RAYMOND	KOSSEN	MARINE AIR WING	KOREA
ARLAND A.	KRAKOW	ARMY S/SGT	PEARL HARBOR WW II
DAVID O.	KRANZ	ARMY	KOREA
MICHAEL	KRAUSE	AF SGT SAC	DESERT STORM-1988-92
PAUL F.	KRAUSE	NAVY MEDIC	WW II 1943-46
EDWARD N.	KRAUSE	ARMY COLONEL	JAPAN-WW II
ROGER	KREITZMAN	AIR FORCE M/SGT.	KOREA & VIETNAM
JAMES	KRONEBUSCH	MARINE PFC.	WW II
LEN.	KRONENBERG	ARMY AIR CORP	CHINA WW II
OLIVER	KRUEGER	ARMY SFC	WW II & KOREA
MARCEL	KRUEGER	ARMY MECHANIC	1955-57
LARRY D	KRUEGER	AIR FORCE	VIETNAM 1967-71
E. W.	KRUSCINSKI	MARINE CORPORAL	IWO JIMA 1943-46
REUBEN C.	KUCK	ARMY COOK CPL.	KOREA 1950-52
LAWRENCE H.	KUCK	ARMY MEDIC CPL.	KOREA 1952-54
RALPH L.	KUCK	ARMY DRIVER PFC.	KOREA 1953-55
O. N. "OTTO"	KUENZI	ARMY SIG. CORP.	JAPAN 1952-54
MARIE	KUENZI	ARMY NURSE CORP	SO. PACIFIC-WWII
ROBERT A	KUENZI	ARMY SGT 32ND DIV	PACIFIC-WW II
PHILIP A.	KUMBA	NAVY MECHANIC	1956-1957
DAN	KURTH	NAVY CPO	1972-1996
LYLE E.	KURTZ	ARMY RADIO OPERATOR	KOREA-1951-52
JACK	KUTCHER	ARMY NAT. GUARD	1947-1990
SCOTT A.	KUTZKE	NATIONAL GUARD E/4	1986-94
BRIAN R	KUTZKE	NAVY CARRIER	VIETNAM 1971-75
ALLEN R	KUTZKE	ARMY T/5	WW II—KOREA
DANIEL P.	KUTZKE	101ST AIRBORNE	VIETNAM 1968-69
ERNIE	KUTZKE SR.	ARMY GUNNER SGT.	WW II
PETER J.	KUZMA	U. S ARMY	TEXAS WW II
DONALD K.	LAABS	ARMY ENGINEER	KOREA 1956-58
ARMIN F.	LAABS SR.	ARMY	ETO-ITALY-WW II
CRYSTAL M.	LAPER	ARMY SPECIALIST	IRAQ 2004-05
RUSS. D.	LARSON	ARMY RADIO OP.	PFC. 1952-54
RUSSELL	LARSON	ARMY MSG INTEL	1980-2001
RICHARD	LARSON	USAF S/SGT.	1946-49
ERNEST W.	LARSON	ARMY MP	KOREA 1955-57
JACK H.	LARSON	ARMY INFANTRY	KOREA 1951-52
LLOYD J.	LATHROP	USAF ACFT MECH	LIBYA 1959-63
ELROY J	LATHROP	USN ACFT MECH	RESERVE 1954-58
THOMAS J.	LAUDE	ARMY ENGR CPT	AFGHANISTAN
GORDON E.	LAUE	AF MECHANIC F 51	KOREAN WAR 1950-52

KENNETH E.	LAUE	ARMY MP	WW II 1945-46
RON	LAUERSDORF	ARMY MECHANIC	VIETNAM
WM. C.	LAURITZEN	NAVY RM/3	KOREA 1955-58
JERRY	LAURITZEN	AIR FORCE	KOREA-1953-1957
ARNOLD E.	LAUTH	US ARMY	PACIFIC WW II 1944-46
ALAN E.	LAUTH	ARMY 25TH INF.	VIETNAM 1969-71
VIRGIL L.	LAUTH	45TH INF. DIVISION	KOREA 1950-52
KEVIN	LAUTH	USMC 5TH COMM	E/4 DESERT STORM
PAUL	LAUTH	ARMY SPC/4	VIETNAM 1965-67
KEITH	LAUTH	MARINE HMM-164	DESERT STORM
C. LAVERTY	LAWS	AF NURSE CAPT	1981-84
P. J.	LEDWOROWSKI	ARMY AIRBORNE	EUROPE-WW II
RICHARD J.	LEECH	ARMY ENGINEER	S/SGT. 1961-67
JOSEPH N.	LEECH	ARMY QM CORP.	P.F.C. WW II
HENRY (BUD)	LEISSES	AIR FORCE PILOT	KIA 1944 PACIFIC WW II
WM. E.	LEISTICO	ARMY SGT 1/C	KOREA 1950-52
E. J.	LEWANDOWSKI	ARMY	POW WW II 1941-45
S. P. K.	LEWIS	BEAVER DAM RIFLES	CIVIL WAR
HARVEY C.	LEWIS	NAVY ETN	VIETNAM 1969-70
ALTON	LIDDICOAT	U. S. NAVY	WW II
LEONARD	LIENKE	ARMY MEDIC SGT.	KOREA 1951-53
FRED. G.	LIENKE	ARMY INFANTRY	FRANCE WW I
EMROY R.	LINDE	ARMY AIR COMBAT	ETO WW II
EMROY R.	LINDE	ARMY AIR COMBAT	GERMANY WW II
DAVID J.	LINK	ARMY SFC.	VIETNAM
HARVEY C.	LINKE	ARMY ENG. T/SGT	ETO WW II 1942-45
DARYL A.	LINKE	ARMY ADMIN. SPEC.	1970-72
RUSSEL	LITSCHER	ARMY 209TH ENGINEER	CBI WW II
G. R.	LIVERSEED	ARMY CB	VIETNAM
ROBERT	LIVERSEED	ARMY TRK DRIVER	WIA-WW II
DOUGLAS L.	LLOYD	MARINE CORPORAL	IWO JIMA WW II
DOUGLAS L.	LLOYD	NAVY CAPTAIN	GULF WAR I
CARLTON L.	LOECK	US ARMY SP/3	KOREA-1954-57
DAVID	LONGFIELD	ARMY ENGINEER	1971-1974
KEN	LONGSETH	MARINE S/SGT.	VIETNAM 1965-66
GORDON D.	LUCK	US ARMY	GERMANY-1954-56
JAMES A.	LUNDE	ARMY MP 1ST CAV.	OCCUPATION 1946-48
DON W.	MACDONALD	USAF MECHANIC	1943-45
JAMES	MACDONALD	ARMY INFANTRY	VIETNAM
HERB	MACHKOVCH	ARMY TANK PFC.	EUROPE WW II
C. JIM	MACHKOVCH	ARMY CPL. 14 DIV.	ETO WW II
BERN.	MACHKOVCH	NAVY PILOT LT.	PACIFIC WW II
RICHARD	MACK	ARMY ENGINEER	KOREA-1953-56
ROBERT	MAHONEY	NAVY AF PILOT	WW II 1942-46
MICHAEL W.	MAIER	NAVY SPX	1944-1946
DONALD R.	MAJORS	NAVY CWO/3	CARRIER-1954-30 YRS
DAVID L.	MALECK	ARMY MISSILE	1965-67
BERNARD	MALLON	CCM NAVY SEABEE	PACIFIC WW II
ROBERT J.	MALY	U.S. AIR FORCE	1961-81
ROBERT J.	MANKE	ARMY RADIO OPER.	PFC. 1971-76
PETER E.	MANLEY	NAVY	WW II 1943-46

JERRY	MANSKE	NAVY YN/2	1951-59
ALEX J.	MANTES	ARMY ENGINEERS	WW II—KOREA
ROBERT	MANTES	AIR FORCE BAND	SGT. WW II
JAMES G.	MANTES	ARMY CAVALRY	1/SGT. WW I
MARJORIE	MANTES	WAC SGT.	VIETNAM
CARL R.	MANTHE	NAVY CPO	WW II & KOREA
MIKE	MARLEFSKI	ARMY WAGONER	WIA WW I
C. R.	MARQUARDT	ARMY PFC	JAPAN-WW II
PETER	MARTENS	ARMY	WW II
WM. A.	MARTHALER	ARMY ENGINEER	SO. PACIFIC WW II
C. "RED"	MARTHALER	AAF S/SGT	CBI WW II 1940-45
GEO.	MARTHALER	ARMM.G. TRNG CTR	WW I
ROBERT	MARTHALER	ARMY INF.	EUROPE WW II
"RUSTY"	MARTHALER	AIR FORCE M/SGT.	VIETNAM EUROPE
JAMES R.	MARTIN	ARMY PFC	KOREA
ANDREW J.	MARTIN	ARMY PFC.	KOREA 1958-60
"CHIP"	MARTINSEN	ARMY MEDIC MSG	1973-1993
DONALD	MATTHEWS	ARMY S/SGT 776TH	PACIFIC WW II
RODGER	MATTSON	AIR FORCE	1971-74
KEN	MATUSESKI	ARMY INF.	GERMANY WW II
WOODROW D.	MAY	ARMY T/5	EUROPE WW II 1942-46
MARLAND "BUD"	MAY	ARMY RADIO OPER	WW II 1942-1946
RONALD	MAYBERRY	ARMY 13TH ARTY	VIETNAM 1965-67
JIM	MCCAMISH JR.	ARMY RADIO COM.	VIETNAM 1966-68
J. R.	MCCAMISH SR.	ARMY MEDIC	KOREA 1940-45
RON M	MCCARTHY	AIR FORCE	1950-1954
KEYS	MCCONAGHY	ARMY ORD. LT.	ETO WW II
LEE J.	MCCONAGHY	AIR FORCE CAPT.	INTELLIGENCE-VIETNAM
PHIL J.	MCDONALD	USAF MECHANIC	KOREA 1951-55
NEIL	MCFAYDEN	ARMY P.F.C. 29INF.	K.I.A. FRANCE WW II
M.	MCGLOTHIN	ARMY SPC.	KIA IRAQ 2004
HARRY	MCKINNEY	MARINE PRIVATE	WW II
ALEX	MCMILLAN	ARMY INFANTRY	CIVIL WAR-1864-65
DANIEL	MCMILLAN	ARMY INFANTRY	FRANCE-WW I
WINSTON D.	MCMILLAN	US ARMY	WW II
MALCOLM	MCMILLAN	US ARMY AIR CORP	WW II 1942-1946
EUGENE	MCMILLAN	ARMY CAPT AIRBORNE	WW II-KOREA-1942-62
R. W.	MCMILLAN	ARMY RIGGER	82ND ABN-1956-58
MORRIS	MCMILLAN	ARMY CPL GUNNER	P.O.W.-PACIFIC-WW II
INEZ	MCMILLAN	ARMY NURSE	WW II 1944-46
DAN M.	MCMILLAN	ARMY AIRBORNE INF	1968-1971
GERALD	MCMILLAN	ARMY ARTILLERY	WW II
JAMES C.	MCMILLAN	MARINE 1940 46	PLATOON SGT—WW II
MICHAEL	MCMILLAN	ARMY TANK	VIETNAM 1969-72
GREG J.	MCMILLAN	AIR FORCE SGT	SECURITY-1969-73
CHRIS M.	MCMILLAN	NAVY ARMY RES.	1969-1999
JIM	MEGALE	ARMY	FRANCE WW I
STEVE	MEGALE	ARMY SIGNAL CORP	WW II
MARTY	MEGALE	ARMY ORDNANCE	KOREA
CHARLES	MERSCH	ARMY SP/5 COOK	VIETNAM 1969-70
JOSEPH W.	MERSCH	ARMY	VIETNAM

ALBERT	MERTZ	NAVY R/ADMIRAL	SPAN/AMER–WW I
DONALD	MESSER	ARMY AF MECHANIC	1957-59
LOREN L	MEYER	NAVY LT COM JG	WW II 1941-42 PACIFIC
TOM P.	MEYER	525TH MP CO.	ARMY 1971-73
WM R.	MICHEL	ARMY SGT	WW II & KOREA
WM. H.	MILARCH	ARMY 1ST/SGT.	WW II 1942-45
RICHARD	MILLER	ARMY MP CPL	WW II 1942-45
JAMES D.	MILLER	AIR FORCE SGT	WW II 1944-46
WALTER	MILLER	NAVY	WW II 1940-46
ROBERT E	MILLER	ARMY	VIETNAM
JOHN E.	MILLER	ARMY 127 INF.	KIA 1918 FRANCE WW I
EUGENE W.	MILLER	USAR SFC.	1952-60
BRUCE E.	MILLER	USAR DRILL SGT.	1974-96
CARL A.	MILLER	ARMY MECHANIC	WW II S/SGT 1941-45
MELVIN L.	MILLER	NAVY BM/2 COX	1943-46
EDWIN J.	MILLER	AIR FORCE S/SGT.	1947-51
J. FRED	MILLER	MARINE SPEC. SERV.	1946-48
LEWIS E.	MILNER	MARINE 1ST DIV.	CHINA 1946
F. B.	MITTELSTADT	ARMY SIGNAL CORP.	WW II 1941-45
JOHN J.	MLODZIK	ARMY M.P.	WW II
WM. D.	MORGAN	U. S. ARMY 2/LT	WW I
DONALD	MORGAN	U. S. NAVY	1952-56
THOMAS G.	MORGAN	COAST GUARD S 1/C	WW II 1942-45
JOSEPH L.	MORSE	ARMY SP/4	1967-68
HAROLD D.	MOYLAN	US ARMY SGT.	1957-63
G. O.	MUEHLENHAUPT	AIR FORCE CADET	WW II 1944-46
F. DALE	MUENCHOW	USAF NAVIGATOR	WW II 1944-46
WM S.	MURPHY JR.	NAVY AOM	PACIFIC WW II
WM. A.	MUSACK	ARMY CPL	KOREA 1953-55
HAROLD	NAGLER	ARMY AIR CORP	WW II
JOHN J.	NEBL	ARMY	S. PACIFIC–WW II
EDWIN E.	NEHLS	ARMY INF. SFC	WIA PH DSC KOREA
RAYMOND	NEHRING	ARMY AIR FORCE	WW II
LEON E.	NEIS	ARMY MORTAR SEC	CPL-KOREA-1953-54
DONNA M.	NEIS	ARMY NURSE SFC	1974-96—GULF WAR I
MERLIN M.	NEIS	NAVY LST	WW II 1944-1946
RAY L.	NEISIUS	ARMY TANK T/4	TUNIS ANZIO WW II
LARRY K.	NEITZEL	NAVY SEABEES	1957-59
JAMES W.	NELSON	ARMY PVT.	TAIWAN 1972-75
WALLACE	NETZER	NAVY SM/1	WW II 1942-46
RON. K.	NEUENDORF	MARINE CPL.	1960-63
ROGER	NEUENDORF	MARINE SGT.	1956-59
GLENN	NEUENDORF	NAVY DESTROYER	CUBAN CRISIS
PAUL	NEUENDORF	ARMY MI	GULF WAR I
F. J. "BUTCH"	NEUMAN	MARINE PFC	WW II 1945-46
ROBERT R.	NEUMAN	MARINE CPL.	WIREMAN WW II
RICHARD A.	NEUMAN	ARMY ENGINEER	1953-1955
PAUL J.	NEUMAN	ARMY CAPTAIN	WW II 1942-1945
T. MIKE	NEUMAN	MARINE L/CPL	VIETNAM 1968-70
CHARLES	NEUMANN	ARMY PFC	FRANCE WW I
LEONARD F.	NEUMANN	ARMY CPL DISABLED	KOREA-1953-55

WILBUR	NEUMANN	ARMY PFC.	KOREA 1952-54
GEO. S.	NIEDERMAIR	ARMY ENGINEERS	EUROPE WW II 43-45
HENRY M.	NOLL	IRON MEN OF METZ	95TH INF. WIA WW II
EUGENE G.	NOLL	MARINE L/CPL	1963-69
FRED H.	NOORDHOF	MARINE	WW II
GENE	NORENBERG	AF FUEL SPECIALIST	COLD WAR-1964-68
ROGER	NORENBERG	ARMY FINANCE	1967-1970
JOHN A.	NOTHEIS	ARMY S/SGT. 27 INF.	PHILIPPINES WW II
BERNIE	NOWICKI	MARINE CPL	1953-55
RUSSEL	OATHOUT	ARMY CORPORAL	W. I. A.-WW I
JOHN T.	OATHOUT	ARMY SP/4	1956-1959
JOHN R.	OATHOUT	ARMY LT. COL	1983-2003
MATT J.	O'BRION	NAVY SEABEES	IRAQ 2003
KATHRYN	O'BRION	ARMY SFC ADMIN.	1978-2000
ROSS	O'BRION	ARMY SP/5 ADMIN	1961-64
JIM	OESTREICHER	US MARINE CORP	1958-1962
CHARLES	OFFERMAN	ARMY SP/4	1956-59
RICHARD	OLLINGER	MARINE PFC	HAWAII, 1954-56
CLIFFORD	OLSEN	MARINE 4TH DIV.	1961-67
THOMAS D.	OLSON	ARMY CORPORAL	GERMANY 1954-56
JACOB B.	OMEN	AIR FORCE POLICE	IRAQ WAR
JOHN F.	OMEN	ARMY SERGEANT	KOREA
FRANKLIN	OMEN	ARMY M/SGT	NEW GUINEA-WW II
DEAN	OPPERMANN	ARMY SPEC. 4	GULF WAR I
DWIGHT B.	OWENS	USAAF T/SGT	1940-45
ANTON L.	PABICH	ARMY	WW II 1942-45
MORRIS	PAGE	NAVY SEAMAN	WW II
L. "SLIP"	PAITRICK	ARMY CORPORAL	WW II
GEORGE	PAITRICK	82ND AIRBORNE	COOK SP/4 1956-59
TERRI	PAITRICK	ARMY SP/4	1978-82
GUST	PAPACOSTA	MARINE	KOREA 1951-54
ALBERT A	PARKER	ARMY	EUROPE WW I 1917-19
LEE WM	PARKER	NAVY RADIOMAN	1942-46
JOHN W.	PASEWALD	NAVY CORPSMAN	VIETNAM
DONALD	PASEWALD	ARMY CPL.	WIA KOREA
HORACE	PATCH	ARMY WIA SHILOH	CIVIL WAR
D. H.	PATZISBERGER	AIR FORCE MECH.	1965-69
R.	PATZLSBERGER	ARMY T/SGT	KOREA 1950-52
IRVIN E.	PAYNE	NAVY SEAMAN 2/C	WW II 1945-46
THOMAS M.	PAYNE	ARMY SP/4	VIETNAM 1969-71
JOHN A.	PEARSON	ARMY MEDIC	WW II
RICHARD	PEARSON	ARMY ENGINEER	WW II 1943-45
CHARLES	PECKHAM	ARMY	EUROPE WW II
ARLO M.	PEDERSON	ARMY POW GUARD	NAT. GUARD & WW II
GERALD	PEDERSON	ARMY AIRBORNE SP/5	GERMANY-VIETNAM
JAMES	PEDERSON	ARMY LT/COLONEL	VIETNAM 1962-68
CHRIS	PEDERSON	NAVY DIVER C.P.O.	1992
STEPH	PEDERSON	ARMY MP MAJOR	1992-2000
DALE M.	PETERSON	MARINE SERGEANT	KOREA
CARL J.	PETRUSHA	ARMY ARTILLERY	COAST WW II 1940-43
DONALD	PETTACK	ARMY PFC	KIA ETO WW II

VICTOR A.	POCIUS	ARMY ENGINEER	SP/5 VIETNAM 1967-70
JOSEPH P.	POCIUS	ARMY SGT.	WW II
EARL A.	POETTER	ARMY	GERMANY 1952-54
ALVIN W	POETTER	ARMY	FT. ORD CA. WW II
HARVEY	POETTER	ARMY AIR FORCE	WW II
HERB. O.	POETTER	ARMY TANK/GUNNER	SO. PACIFIC WW II
HERBERT	POLSIN	ARMY ORD. EVAC.	WW II 1943-45
GEORGE C.	POWELL	ARMY INFANTRY	CIVIL WAR
WILLIAM	POWELL	ARMY	FRANCE WW I
DONALD D.	POWELL	ARMY WW II	NAVY KOREA
WM. H.	POWELL	ARMY SGT.	WW II
THOMAS C.	POWELL	NAVY DD729	VIETNAM
"DOC"	PRITCHARD	ARMY ENGINEER	EUROPE WW II
DONALD G.	PROPST	MARINE CPL.	VIETNAM
R. R.	PTASCHINSKI	NAVY COMMISSARY	PO 2/C WW II
RAY	PTASCHINSKI	ARMY M/SGT	WW II
G. N.	PTASCHINSKI	8TH ARMY	JAPAN 1946-48
CLYDE J.	PURVIS	NAVY SUBMARINE	MISSILE T/2 1968-77
CLAYTON	PURVIS	ARMY SGT 168TH INF	ITALY-WW II
JOHN J.	RABATA	AIR FORCE SGT	1949-1952
JAMES R.	RADIG	NAVY/ARMY CWO/4	1948-1989
RICK	RADIG	ARMY ENGINEER	1975-1977
ROBERT	RADIG SR.	113TH ARMY BAND	1984-1990
DUANE A.	RADKE	USAF MECH. M/SGT	SERVED 1955-76
DENNIS M	RADTKE	AIR FORCE S/SGT	1963-1972
LAWRENCE W	RAKE	ARMY 3RD INF	WW II-1941-45
STEPHEN A.	RAKE	101ST AIRBORNE	VIETNAM 1969-70
EDGAR V.	RAMSEUR	ARMY SGT.	WW II
DOUGLAS	RANDALL	ARMY MP LT. COL	SERVED 1953-73
DEWEY N.	RANICH	ARMY MP	PACIFIC WW II
INEZ E.	RANICH	NAVY NURSE LT.	WW II
BRUCE	RASMUSSEN	ARMY CAPTAIN	WIA PACIFIC WW II
GUSTAVE	RAU	ARMY	FRANCE WW I
CLARENCE M.	RAU	AIR FORCE S/SGT	EUROPE WW II
WILLIAM	RAWLSKY	ARMY PILOT CAPT.	VIETNAM
LYLE L.	RAYMOND	ARMY ENGINEER	WW II 1942-46
HARVEY W.	RECHEK	ARMY INF. CPL.	1954-62
STENCIL F.	RECHEK	ARMY M. GUNNER	WW I
STANLEY J.	RECHEK	U. S. ARMY M/SGT.	1946-1988-RETIRED
FRANCIS D.	RECHEK	DRILL SGT. SFC.	USAR-1960-68
ROBERT J.	REEDY	NAVY SEAMAN 1/C	WW II 1945-46
RANDALL	REIBLE	NAVY	JAPAN WW II
JOSEPH J.	REIDER	ARMY ORD. DEPT.	WW II-1943-46
NORMAN H.	REIER	ARMY	PANAMA WW II
"HOD" J.	REIF	ARMY A/B ENGINEER	EUROPE-WW II
JOE E.	REIHBANDT	ARMY PFC.	WORLD WAR II
A. A.	REIHBANDT	SGT 457 TANK CO.	WW II 1943-1945
EMIL	REIHBANDT	ARTILLERY CPL	EUROPE-WW I
W.	REIHBRANDT	ARMY PFC.	WW II
ALVIN	REINHARD	ARMY 632ND TDB	SO. PACIFIC WW II
DAVID F.	REINKE	ARMY ENGINEER	1954-1956

DAVID	RENNHACK	ARMY PFC. AMMO	KOREA 1959-64
RALPH	RENNHACK	ARMY MEDIC PFC.	KOREA 1956-58
DON C.	RENNHACK	ARMY SGT.	1947-48 1952-54
JUNIOR	RENNHACK	ARMY PFC.	WW II 1945-46
HOWARD	RENNHACK	82ND AIRBORNE	SGT. 1950-53
DR. W.	RICHARDS	NAVY PHM 2/C	WW II
DAVE	RICHARDSON	NAVY AIR FORCE	WW II
M. G.	RICHARDSON	ARMY NG AR LTC	1950-76
DANIEL P.	RIEDER	NAVY DESTROYER	WW II-1943-46
ORVILLE H.	RIEGE	ARMY	1952-54
LEO	RIEHBRANDT	ARMY 81ST INF. REG.	KOREA 1951-53
JOHN	RIEHBRANDT	ARMY STAFF SGT.	KOREA 1953-60
E.	RIEHBRANDT JR.	ARMY SGT.	PACIFIC WW II
ROBERT C.	RITSCH	ARMY MEDIC D.D.S.	CAPT. WW II 1943-46
WILLARD	ROBERTS	AAF MECH CPL.	SO. PACIFIC WW II
EARL W.	ROBERTS	ARMY GATE GUARD	GERMANY 1554-57
ROGER K.	ROEBKE	ARMY INFANTRY	GERMANY-1951-53
H. J.	ROGGENBAUER	ARMY MEDIC	WW II 1940-45
HERMAN	ROHRBECH	ARMY 6TH INF.	SPAN-AMER 1898
JOSEPH	ROMAN	US MARINE CORP	VIETNAM 1957-77
MONICA G.	ROMAN	NAVY NURSE LT/CDR	1980-84 & 1989-99
DON.	ROSENMEIER	NAVY HA/1	WW II
DONALD	RUECKERT	NAVY CAREER	1943-1973
CLARENCE	RUPNOW	ARMY M. P. ESCORT	EUROPE-1942-45
FRANK F.	RUSHLOW	ARMY PVT	WW I
JAMES A.	RUSHLOW	ARMY SP/4	BERLIN BLOCKADE
CLINTON G.	RUX	ARMY SGT	KOREA
STAN. B.	SADOSKI	ARMY	WW I
PETER	SCHAALMA	ARMY AIRBORNE CPL	POW-WW II-1944-45
J. D.	SCHACHTNER	ARMY ENGINEER	VIETNAM 1970-71
ROGER A.	SCHAUER	ARMY RADIO OP.	GERMANY 1959-62
LAWRENCE	SCHAUS	ARMY INF	GERMANY WW II
JOE A.	SCHEGETZ	NAVY	KOREA 1950-54
BOB	SCHEGETZ	NAVY	KOREA 1951-55
JOS.	SCHELTER JR.	ARMY	KOREA-BERLIN CRISIS
B. W. "BOZO"	SCHEPP	ARMY ORD. DISPOSAL	SFC KOREA
HAROLD P.	SCHEPP	NAVY MM 1/C	PHILIPPINES-WW II
DANIEL G.	SCHEPP	ARMY COOK	WW II
KEN.	SCHINDEL	ARMY MORTAR SQD	KOREA 1956-57
CAROL M.	SCHINGO	NAVY HOSPITAL	TEXAS WW II
ROBERT	SCHLICHER	ARMY PFC	WW II
WALTER	SCHLIEWE	QM VFW POST 1163	WW 2
LEWIS E.	SCHMELING	ARMY CLERK	1953-55
WERNER J.	SCHMID	ARMY CPL. 95TH MP	WW II
EMIL A.	SCHMID	MERCHANT MARINE	WW II
RICHARD F.	SCHMID	NAVY GUNNER	KOREA-1952-1956
JACK	SCHMIDT	NAVY ELECTRICIAN	1955-57
JAMES J.	SCHMIDT	ARMY INFANTRY	1953-55
DENNIS	SCHMIDT	AIR FORCE S/SGT.	VIETNAM 8TH SOS
LESLIE	SCHMIDT	USAF RADAR OP	KOREA 1953-54
DALE R.	SCHMIDT	COAST GUARD CAPT	1955-84

REUBEN	SCHMIDT	ARMY PFC	EUROPE 1942-45
EUGENE	SCHMIDT	USAF M/SGT RET	BRONZE STAR VIETNAM
RAY C.	SCHMIDT	ARMY	PACIFIC WW II 1942-45
LESTER	SCHMIDT	ARMY CPL.	WIA KOREA
ROBERT	SCHMITT	AF MECHANIC	1952-56
LEO E.	SCHMITT	ARMY CORPORAL	KOREA 1953-55
RAYMOND J.	SCHMITT	ARMY HEAVY EQUIP.	KOREA-1951-53
GREG	SCHMITT	NAVY GMT/2	1977-81
WM	SCHNEIDER	INF. DRUMMER BOY	CIVIL WAR
SYL J.	SCHNEIDER	ARMY MEDIC	EUROPE—WWII
AL. G.	SCHNEIDER	ARMY AIR FORCE	WW II
ORV. W.	SCHNEIDER	ARMY	WW II
ART F.	SCHNEIDER	ARMY AIR FORCE	WW II—VIETNAM
WM G.	SCHNEIDER	ARMY AIR FORCE	WW II
HARV.	SCHOEFFEL	ARMY TRANS CORP	GERMANY 1945-47
EUGENE	SCHOEFFEL	NAVY S/1ST/CLASS	ARMED GUARD-WW II
BOB	SCHOENBERGER	ARMY SGT.	WW II 1945-47
JOHN	SCHOENFELD	ARMY	VIETNAM
BUD	SCHOENWETTER	ARMY INF. SGT.	SPEC. SERVICES-1943-45
HOWARD J.	SCHOENWETTER	SCHOENWETTER	AIR CORP WW II
R.	SCHOENWETTER	AIR FORCE S/SGT.	KOREA-1951-54
EDWARD E.	SCHOLZ	ARMY CORPORAL	PACIFIC-WW II
RICHARD	SCHRAM	AIR FORCE A1/C	KOREA
JAMES	SCHULTEIS	AIR FORCE S/SGT	KOREA—VIETNAM
DONALD	SCHULTZ	USAF MECHANIC	KOREA-1951-55
CARL W.	SCHULTZ	ARMY PFC	ETO WIA WW II
ALVIN W.	SCHULTZ	ARMY	WW II
GORDON A.	SCHULTZ	ARMY SP/4	1955-57
EARL W.	SCHULTZ	ARMY INF.	KOREA
REUBEN	SCHULTZ	ARMY INFANTRY	WW II 1942-46
HARVEY C.	SCHULTZ	ARMY SGT.	BERLIN BLOCKADE
DEL	SCHULTZ	MARINE SCOUT	SNIPER WW II
CHARLES	SCHULZ	ARMY AIRBORNE	1953-55
W. E.	SCHUMACHER	MARINE M/GUNNER	PACIFIC WW II
EDMUND J.	SCHUMANN	ARMY	WW II
RONALD	SCHUSTER	NAVY MACHINIST	1953-57
LORENCE	SCHUSTER	MARINE FLD COOK	WW II 1943-46
STEVEN	SCHUSTER	ARMY HELO PILOT	CW/2 VIETNAM
ROBERT	SCHUSTER	ARMY CSM	1957-98
MARVIN H.	SCHUTTE	ARMY MEDIC	WW II 1943-46
ERVIN W.	SCHUTTE	NAVY MM 2/C	WW II 1943-45
LES A.	SCHWANDT	ARMY SP/5	VIETNAM
WM. M.	SCHWANDT	ARMY PVT	WW I
W. J.	SCHWANTES	NAVY EMC SW CPO	1987-2007
CLIFF R	SCHWARTZ	AIR FORCE CONST	KOREA 1946-47
WILBUR	SCHWARTZ	ARMY	KOREA
PHIL J.	SCHWARTZ	ARMY CREW CHIEF	VIETNAM
JAMES	SCHWEFEL	USAF PILOT CAPT	VIETNAM 1963-70
WM C.	SCHWEIGER	ARMY MP	ETO WW II
LES C.	SCHWOCH	ARMY INF.	KOREA 1952-54
WALTER	SEEGERT	SEAMAN 1ST/CLASS	NAVY-WW II

ROB'T L.	SEERING	ARMY CAVALRY	SO. PACIFIC WW II
ALFRED C	SEERING	ARMY	FRANCE WWI
VERNON	SEHLOFF	NAVY ENGINEER	PACIFIC WW II 1943-46
ROBERT R.	SEIPPEL	ARMY KIA WW II	D.A.V. CHAPTER 50
PETER J.	SEIPPEL	USAR 1/ LT.	19??-1972
CHARLES E.	SELL	NAVY CARRIER 31	KOREA 1950-53
BRIAN C.	SELL	ARMY	1976-79
JOE	SENNEFF	QM VFW POST 1163	WW I
WALTON L.	SETHER	AF MECHANIC	WW II
BURTON L.	SHEPARD	ARMY MEDIC	ETO WW II 1942-46
RAY M.	SHERLOCK	AIR FORCE	ENGLAND 1948-54
HENRY G.	SHERMAN	3622 ORDNANCE CO.	ALASKA 1950-52
ART.	SHERMAN JR.	ARMY HQ 141 P.F.C.	K.I.A. FRANCE WW II
JAMES J.	SHESKEY	ARMY T/5	WW II ERA 1946-48
RODNEY	SHESKEY	US COAST GUARD	WORLD WAR II
HAROLD E.	SHUTE	ARMY T/5 1941-45	PEARL HARBOR WW II
JEFFERY L.	SHUTE	ARMY PFC	VIETNAM 1971-73
GEORGE	SIEJA	ARMY SIGNAL CORP.	ITALY EUROPE WW II
EDWARD F.	SIEJA	ARMY CO. E	128TH INF. WW II
JOSEPH W.	SIRES	ARMY RANGE NCO	PANAMA-WW II
JOHN T.	SIRES	ARMY MEDIC	VIETNAM-1965-71
DOUGLAS J.	SIRES	ARMY MEDIC	AFGHANISTAN-2000-08
CARL C.	SLADE	ARMY INF. PFC	KOREA-1951-53
DEL.	SLINGER	NAVY FIREMAN 1/C	PACIFIC-WW II
ERNEST	SLOVAK	ARMY INFANTRY	WW II 1942-46
GORDON D.	SMITH	NAVY RADIOMAN	WW II 1943-46
GERALD R.	SMITH	ARMY SFC.	WW II KOREA
NORMAN E.	SMITH	NAVY S/1C	WW II 1943-46
LAWRENCE W	SMITH	ARMY CORPORAL	KOREA
GARY L.	SMITH	ARMY SP/4	VIETNAM 1972-74
LYLE N.	SMITH	ARMY SGT.	ETO WW II 1944-46
NEWTON	SMITH	NAVY S2	WW I
DONALD R	SMITH	ARMY T/5 ORD	EUROPE 1942-45
DENNIS L.	SMITH	ARMY INFANTRY	WIA VIETNAM
VIRGIL R.	SMITH	ARMY ENGINEER	WW II 1943-1946
F. J.	SOMMERCORN	NAVY PILOT LT	S. PACIFIC-WW II
DICK	SOUTHWORTH	ARMY PFC.	KOREA 1953-55
HAROLD	SPIEL	U. S.ARMY MEDIC	ITALY-WW II
THOS. E.	SPRAGUE	ARMY MAJOR	DESERT STORM
PERCIVAL	SPRAGUE	ARMY AIR FORCE	PACIFIC WW II
MERLIN P.	SPROTTE	MARINE CORP	PACIFIC-1943-46
CHARLES	STAAB	NAVY YEOMAN	VIETNAM 1966-70
BRENDA L.	STACEY	NAVY SHCMCMC	1982-05
WILLIAM J.	STAM	NAVY P.C.	VIETNAM
CLARENCE	STANGE	ARMY CPL.	KOREA-1950-52
JIM	STANGE	ARMY SP/4 CLERK	GERMANY 1973-74
R. R. "BOB"	STANGL	NAVY	WW II
BEN C.	STANGL	ARMY ARTILLERY	PACIFIC WW II
HAROLD F	STAPEL	ARMY AIR FORCE S/SGT	WW II 1942-45
CHAS. E.	STARKS	U. S. ARMY M/SGT	WW II-KOREA-30 YRS
CECIL H.	STEBBINS	AIR FORCE	WW II 1944-45

HARVEY H.	STEBBINS	ARMY WAGONER	WW I 1917-19
ALVIN C.	STEFFEN	ARMY RETIREE	WW II-KOREA-VIETNAM
JAMES	STEGER SR.	MARINE	VIETNAM
HOWARD	STEGNER	ARNG USAR MAJOR	BERLIN BLOCKADE
GEO. F.	STEGNER	ARMY	KOREA 1953-55
JOSEPH	STEHLING	ARNG B/GENERAL	1932 WWII 1970
HENRY J.	STEHLING	USAF B/GENERAL	1942-70
S. C.	STEHLING	ARMY 1ST/LT	1970-1977
FRED J.	STEHLING	WIS ANG HQ M/SGT	1966-1986
JOSEPH	STEHLING JR.	ARMY ENGINEER	1960-85 (RVN)
ALLEN	STEINER	AIR FORCE 1965 69	VIETNAM 1967-69
HERBERT	STERN	ARMY MP T/5	ALEUTIANS 1942-45
PAUL	STERRENBERG	AIR FORCE SGT. E/5	1968-72
DR. C.	STERRENBERG	NAVY DENTIST	WW II 1942-1946
BERNARD	STOFFLET	ARMY	WW II 1943-45
DALE J.	STONE	MARINE CORPORAL	1978-82
EDGAR T.	STONE JR.	AIR FORCE M/SGT.	1977-94 RET.
JOSEPH S.	STORTZ	NAVY BM 2/C	PACIFIC WW II 1943-46
RICHARD	STORTZ	NAVY FORRESTAL	ATLANTIC 1968-70
STEPHEN A.	STORTZ	ARMY CPL. INF.	KOREA 1951-53
ROBERT	STOWELL	ARMY S/4 ARTY	1964-70
KIRK	STRASESKIE	MARINE SGT.	DIED IRAQ 5/19/2003
D. J.	STRIEFF III	MARINE CORPORAL	1971-1973
D. J.	STRIEFF JR.	ARMY MP	WW II 1945-46
G. H.	STROHBUSCH SR.	NAVY	KOREA
TIM M.	STRUBE	NAVY E/5	VIETNAM 1968-71
DONALD G.	STRUBE	MARINE CPL.	VIETNAM 1965-67
N.	STRUMBERGER	ARMY 555TH AA	WW II 1942-45
ROBERT	SUGDEN	ARMY	KOREA—1953-55
ROBERT	SUKOWSKI	ARMY ENGINEER	EUROPE WW II
EDWARD	SUSTMAN	MARINE S/SGT	WW II PHILIPPINES
DONNA M.	SUTTON	WAF S/SGT RCTG	1950-1952
ROBERT F.	SUTTON	USAF MACHINIST	1952-1956
CHARLES	SWAIN SR.	ARMY RANGER P.F.C.	SO. PACIFIC WW II
DENNIS W.	SWAN	AIRFORCE A I/C	KOREA 1952-57
DICK	TABB	MARINE SGT.	1954-60
ROBERT	TABB	MARINE SGT.	1980-87
MARK	TABB	NAVY GSM/2	1993-97
STANLEY	TADYCH	ARMY INF SP/3	ALASKA 1955-57
HARRY J.	TANK JR.	ARMY 517 AMFA	GERMANY 1953-55
GERALD	TELETZKE	ARMY MAJOR CE	FAR EAST 1946-49
"STONEY"	TELETZKE	ARMY	FRANCE WW I
LOUIS	TEMKIN	ARMY PFC	WW II
JULIUS	TEMKIN	ARMY SP/3	KOREA
SAM	TEMKIN DDS	ARMY MAJOR	WW II
MARK	TEMKIN MD	ARMY MAJOR	WW II
RAYMOND J.	THIEL	MARINE S/SGT	1949-52 INC. KOREA
DAVID R.	THOMAS	ARMY CORPORAL	KOREA 1951-53
LES. J.	TIEDT	ARMY SPEC. 4	1963-69
RONALD R.	TIEDT	ARMY MEDIC	1964-69
MELVIN	TIELENS	15TH AF PILOT B 25	1ST/LT ITALY WW II

RAYMOND A.	TIETZ	ARMY S/SGT	WW II
DONALD	TILLEMA	AIR FORCE SGT	KOREA 1951-55
ALAN J.	TISDALE	ARMY MEDIC	VIETNAM 1970-71
ALVIN	TOELLNER	ARMY S/SGT	WW II 1941-46
GERALD	TOLSMA	ARMY MECHANIC	KOREA 1951-53
DICK	TOMASHEK	NAVY	KOREA 1949-53
MICHAEL G.	TRAPP	USAR COOK	1962-68
THOMAS	TRATAR	MARINE CORPORAL	PACIFIC 1944-46
G. R.	TRIEMSTRA	ARMY ENGINEER	KOREA-1951-53
LLOYD E.	TUCKER	NAVY SEABEE	WW II
ALFRED R.	TUCKER	ARMY SGT. MAJOR	1940-81
LEVI N.	TURNER	ARMY LT. WIA	CIVIL WAR 1863
H. C.	TWARDOKUS	ARMY	WW I
LEE K.	VAUGHAN	AIR FORCE AMMS	VIETNAM 1966-69
A. F. (BUD)	VELING	ARMY	WW II-1943
MERLE	VERRIDEN	TANK MECHANIC	FRANCE WW II
ROBERT	VETTER	AIR FORCE LT.	KILLED MISS. WW II
C. C.	VINSIAUSKI	AIR FORCE 2/LT.	WW II
EARL R.	VOCKROTH	NAVY AMM 2/C	WW II 1942-45
ERROL E.	VOELKER	NAVY	WW II
MERLIN H.	VOIGT	ARMY MECHANIC	GERMANY
ROBERT	VOIGT	NAVY MEDIC	1984-88
ART. "TOM"	VORPAHL	5TH AF SERV. SQDN	PACIFIC-WW II
HAROLD C.	VOSEKUIL	ARMY MP S/4	VIETNAM 1966-67
HARRY G	VOSEKUIL	ARMY HALF-TRACK	WIA ETO 1942-45
DON. L.	VOSEKUIL	ARMY 73RD ABN BDE	VIETNAM 1965-66
KEN E.	WADDELL	ARMY MESS SGT.	2ND DIV. KOREA
DUANE R.	WADE	ARMY SECURITY	KOREA—1958-1961
EUGENE	WADLEIGH	US ARMY	KOREA
V. J.	WADLEIGH	ARMY	GERMANY 1956-58
MELVIN	WAGNER	ARMY	WW II
GERALD W.	WAGNER	NAVY RADIO UDT	1963-67
FRITZ W.	WAGNER	NAVY ARMED GUARD	WW II
JEREMY G.	WALKER	ARMY AVIATION	GULF WAR II
RHIM C.	WALKER	ARMY CW/3	GULF WAR I & II
JOLEEN J.	WALKER	ARMY CSM	IRAQI FREEDOM
ELMER G.	WALTERS	NAVY SEAMEN 2/C	WIA-PACIFIC-WW II
MICHAEL	WAPNESKI	MARINE CPL E/4	1971-75
JOE. N.	WAPNESKI	ARMY T/5	WW II
JOE. P.	WAPNESKI	ARMY INF. PVT.	WW I
JEFFREY	WARMKA	AIR FORCE SRA	1982-1986
NICHOLAS	WEAVER	CORNELL BRIG. PVT.	REVOLUTION 1778
PAUL	WEBER	ARMY 5TH RCT CPL.	KOREA 1953
TED	WEBER	ARMY 24TH DIV. CPL.	KOREA 1953-55
ROB'T D.	WEBSTER	ARMY INFANTRY	PACIFIC WW II
RONALD	WEGENER	NAVY RD2 E/5	1959-65
HARVEY H.	WEGNER	USS EARL JOHNSON	DE702 NAVY WW II
LEO G.	WEHNER	ARMY INFANTRY	KOREA 1952-54
L.	WEINGARTEN	MARINE 5TH DIV.	WIA PACIFIC WW II
DELMAR E.	WENDT	ARMY PFC.	KIA 12/10/42 WW II
ORVILLE	WENDT	ARMY 32ND DIV.	PACIFIC WW II

RALPH	WERBELOW	ARMY SP/3 FDC	GERMANY 1954-56
WALT.	WERSLAWSKE	ARMY PFC	FRANCE-WW I
GERALD F.	WERTH	AIR FORCE PILOT	1969-2000
PETER S.	WESTRA	NAVY	KOREA 1952-56
ROBT L.	WHEELER	ARMY 5TH RTC	COMBAT-KOREA
M. DEAN	WHEELER	MARINE 1ST DIV.	1953-1957
STEPHEN J.	WHITE	AIR FORCE M/SGT.	1971-91
HENRY A.	WHITE	NAVY S 1/C	WW II 1944-46
RICHARD F.	WHITE	AIR FORCE T/SGT	KOREA-1948-54
ROBERT N.	WHITE	ARMY INFANTRY	VIETNAM 1969-71
NOLAND R.	WHITE	ARMY SUPPLY	PANAMA WW II
JACK W.	WHITE	ARMY INF. SGT.	VIETNAM 1967-69
RANDY	WICHINSKI	AIR FORCE	1972-75
GORDON	WIEGERT	ARMY SUPPLY SGT.	1950-52
AMIL G.	WIENKE	PVT. PROV REGT	WORLD WAR I
WALTER R.	WIERSMA	ARMY 385TH SIGNAL	VIETNAM 1966-68
ROBERT	WIERSMA	ARMY 67TH GUN BN.	WW II 1942-45
LARRY L.	WIERSMA	ARMY INFANTRY	VIETNAM 1967-69
ROMAN G.	WILD	NAVY	WW II
BENJAMIN W.	WILD	AIR FORCE SGT	WW II-1942-45
IRVIN	WILLIAMS	NAVY MACH MATE	KOREA 1952-55
OWEN H.	WILLIAMS	ARMY SERGEANT	WW I 1917-18
GAIL G.	WILLIAMS	ARMY	WW II
WARREN	WILLIAMS	ARMY CPL COOK	1951-53
C. G.	WILLIHNGANZ	NAVY AIR CREWMAN	WW II-1943-46
SAL	WILLIHNGANZ	ARMY CO.E 32D DIV.	WW II 1941-1945
WM. "BILL"	WILTSE	NAVY USS MIDWAY	KOREA 1953-57
LYLE L.	WINKER	ARMY CORPORAL	1952-54
DELMAR	WINNING	USAF PHOTO RECON	WW II 1943-45
MARVIN E.	WINTER	ARMY ARTILLERY	WW II 1943-45
EDWARD E.	WINTER	STOREKEEPER	NAVY 1959-63
ALAN M.	WINTER	STATE COMMANDER	VFW MAINE 1993-94
LAWRENCE E	WINTER	ARMY AIR FORCE	1943-1945
EDW.	WISKOWSKI	ARMY	KIA-WW II
JIM	WISNIEWSKI	AIR FORCE S/SGT.	1968-1972
ARNOLD R.	WODILL	US ARMY INFANTRY	KOREA
CLARENCE	WOLC	MARINE SGT	1954-57
RODNEY W	WOLC	ARMY COMSET	1976-82
VIRG.	WOLLENBURG	NAVY	WW II 1943-46
WARD P.	WOLTMAN	ARMY INF. PFC.	PACIFIC WW II
DONALD	WOODS SR.	AIR FORCE	VIETNAM
JOHN	WRZESINSKE	ARMY SP/3	1956-58
JOHN	WRZESINSKE	MARINE	WW I
DICK	WRZESINSKI	ARMY AIR CORP	WW II-1943-46
FRANK	WRZESINSKI	ARMY	FRANCE-WW I
ADAM	WUESTHOFF	USMC INF	IRAQ
FLOYD	YAGER	AAF S/SGT 1505	KIA WW II
G. L.	YAGODINSKI	ARMY INFANTRY	KOREA-1952-54
ELROY A.	YAROCH	AAF GUNNER B 17	ETO-W.I.A-P.O.W.-WW II
PAUL J.	YASGER	US ARMY	KOREA
P. N.	YOUNGDALE	ARMY 25TH DIV.	JAPAN WW II

MAJ. D. J.	YOUNGDALE	AIR FORCE PILOT	1989-CAREER
WILLIAM	YUENGER	MARINE CPL. E/4	WIA VIETNAM 65-68
DONALD A.	ZABEL	MARINE CORPORAL	VIETNAM 1967-68
ROBERT L.	ZAMZOW	AIR FORCE SP E5	1968-72
DONALD H.	ZEATLOW	101 AIRBORNE MEC.	VIETNAM
ANDREW	ZEHREN	USAAF SGT	AFRICA-WW II
CARLTON	ZELLAR	ARMY FIRST SGT.	1953-93
DREW D.	ZELLE	WIS. GUARD 1/SGT	OP. IRAQ 2005-06
FRED E.	ZEMP	ARMY INF. PFC	WIA EUROPE 1944-45
ERWIN W.	ZICK JR.	AIR CORP WW II	WIARNG CDR.
EARL	ZIEMAN	AIR FORCE PILOT	WW II
DONALD	ZILEWICZ	AIR FORCE	VIETNAM 1968-74
DONALD	ZILISCH	101ST AIRBORNE	ARMY-VIETNAM
PHILIP J.	ZINK	CO. K COLONEL	WW I
DOUGLAS	ZIVNEY	ARMY 32ND DIVISION	WIA PACIFIC WW II
DELMAR	ZUEHLKE	ARMY S/SGT CLERK	PACIFIC-WW II

It is my hope your life has been greatly enhanced by sharing a moment in the life of a soldier.

THE 15,000 PEOPLE OF THIS COMMUNITY BUILT A VETERAN'S MEMORIAL PARK AND INCLUDED A MEMORIAL AND WARRIOR WALLS WITH THE HISTORY OF EACH VETERAN ENGRAVED IN BLACK GRANITE.

THEY ALSO CREATED A VETERAN'S MUSEUM IN THE DODGE COUNTY HISTORICAL SOCIETY BUILDING TO DOCUMENT THE COURAGE OF LOCAL VETERANS AND TO EXHIBIT FOR ALL TO SEE ACTUAL MILITARY LIFE OF THIS COMMUNITY.

THE AUTHOR DONATED TEN YEARS OF WORK; COLLECTING AND RECORDING LOCAL VETERANS STORIES GIVING THEM TO THIS MUSEUM SO CHILDREN OF THE FUTURE CAN RESEARCH THIS RICH RESOURCE.

VETERAN'S MUSEUM

DODGE COUNTY HISTORICAL SOCIETY — VETERAN'S MUSEUM

AMERICAN LEGION POST 146 VETERAN'S CENTER

THE AUTHOR OF THIS BOOK IS AN ADVOCATE FOR THE AVERAGE SOLDIER AND DEVOTED OVER TEN YEARS OF HIS RETIREMENT DAYS TO HONORING THE TYPICAL MAN OR WOMAN WARRIOR. IT IS VITALLY IMPORTANT TO HIM THAT CHILDREN OF THE NEXT GENERATIONS RESPECT, HONOR, AND REMEMBER THOSE WHO PRESERVE OUR FUTURE.

THE AUTHOR (A VETERAN) USED THE WORDS AND THOUGHTS OF MANY WARRIORS TO PLACE THIS BOOK OF WISDOM IN FRONT OF YOU AND MAKES NO CLAIM TO BE ORIGINAL.

THESE WORDS ARE SPOKEN IN MANY ACCENTS BY TENS OF THOUSANDS AND THE PICTURES DEPICT HUNDREDS OF THOUSANDS SOME OF WHOM GRIEVE FOR THEIR MISSING LIMBS OR PRAY FOR A PEACEFUL STATE OF MIND IN THE DARK OF NIGHT. YOU CANNOT PUT A COPY-WRITE ON A SOLDIERS FEELINGS NOR A PATENT ON THEIR WOUNDS, BUT YOU CAN GIVE THEM HEALING RESPECT!

RESPECTFULLY WRITTEN BY;
ROBERT (BOB) FRANKENSTEIN